The Best
30-Minute
Vegetarian
Recipes

The Best
30-Minute
Vegetarian
Recipes

Marie-Claude Morin

Robert
ROSE

The Best 30-Minute Vegetarian Recipes
Text copyright © 2011 Marie-Claude Morin
Photographs copyright © 2009 Headlight
   Les Publications Modus Vivendi Inc.
   55 rue Jean-Talon Ouest, 2nd floor
   Montreal (Quebec) H2R 2W8
Cover and text design copyright © 2011 Robert Rose Inc.

For complete cataloguing information, see page 182.

Disclaimer

The recipes in this book have been carefully tested by our kitchen and our tasters. To the best of
our knowledge, they are safe and nutritious for ordinary use and users. For those people with food
or other allergies, or who have special food requirements or health issues, please read the suggested
contents of each recipe carefully and determine whether or not they may create a problem for you.
All recipes are used at the risk of the consumer.

We cannot be responsible for any hazards, loss or damage that may occur as a result of any
recipe use.

For those with special needs, allergies, requirements or health problems, in the event of any
doubt, please contact your medical adviser prior to the use of any recipe.

Design and Production: Joseph Gisini/PageWave Graphics Inc.
Editor: Carol Sherman
Recipe Editor: Jennifer MacKenzie
Copy Editor: Jo Calvert
Translator: Donna Vekteris
Photography: David Radburn and André Rozon; studio de photographie Headlight
Prop and Food Stylists: Marie-Claude Morin, André Rozon and David Radburn

Cover: Vegetable Stir-Fry (page 127)
Page 2: Eggplant with Tomato (page 151)
Page 5: Mango Salad (page 76) and Bread Salad (page 77)
Page 6: Divine Salad (page 68)
Page 8: Warm Potato Salad (page 75) and Russian Salad (page 74)
Page 9: Greek Salad (page 61)

We acknowledge the financial support of the Government of Canada through the Book Publishing
Industry Development Program (BPIDP) for our publishing activities.

Published by Robert Rose Inc.
120 Eglinton Avenue East, Suite 800, Toronto, Ontario, Canada M4P 1E2
Tel: (416) 322-6552 Fax: (416) 322-6936
www.robertrose.ca

Printed and bound in Canada

1 2 3 4 5 6 7 8 9 MP 19 18 17 16 15 14 13 12 11

Marie-Claude Morin

A host on radio station RockDétente in the Outaouais region of
Quebec, Canada, and a mother of three, Marie-Claude Morin
offers you the fruits of her culinary adventures.

Contents

Introduction 10

Appetizers 17

Soups 41

Salads 57

Main Dishes 83

Sides 139

Desserts 157

Index 183

Here's an English edition of
The Best 30-Minute Vegetarian Recipes.
This is good news! It means there are many
of you out there ready to go vegetarian.
Maybe for a day, maybe forever.
Enjoy!

Introduction

Do You Want to Eat Well?

Do you want to eat healthy foods? Do you want to simplify your life? You can. We tend to think of vegetarian cooking as a complex adventure. This book will prove the opposite. I'm a vegetarian. I follow my instincts. I like to eat well. And, perhaps like you, I'm a mother on the run who juggles work, family and food. I learned to cook quickly. The minutes we save in the kitchen can be used to listen to our children tell us about their day, to have discussions with our friends or to gaze into our loved ones' eyes. We must appreciate the beautiful things and the good things in life. *The Best 30-Minute Vegetarian Recipes* is intended not only for vegetarians but also for people who would like to try eating vegetarian from time to time.

Variety

Some people are born vegetarians, some become vegetarians over time, and others just like to eat this way now and then. We eat vegetarian for all kinds of reasons: for taste, by desire, on principle and out of respect. We have to feel free to be a vegetarian according to what feels right. You'll see that vegetarian cuisine is very imaginative. Among the legumes, tofu, cereal grains, fruits and vegetables, there's a wide range of possibilities. It's true, you have to put a little effort into it, but the result is a varied, colorful and inviting diet.

Simplicity and Speed

We often rack our brains for nothing. The simple things are usually the best. Flavors take full effect in simplicity, and this book is meant to be unpretentious. The lists of ingredients are not very long and the steps for following recipes are easy. *The Best 30-Minute Vegetarian Recipes* contains many recipes invented under pressure to calls of "I'm hunnnnnnngry...". It contains many of the great classics revisited, several family jewels that have been handed down and a few of my own personal treasures. Some recipes demand a little more time, but, in general, they can be made in less than 30 minutes.

Accessibility

It's often happened to me that I was leafing through inspiring cookbooks, and then got discouraged when I read the list of ingredients. That's what made me want to offer you a cookbook that's accessible. You won't have to run to specialty food stores to find this or that ingredient. You'll find absolutely everything you need just about everywhere. What you won't find in this book is nutritional information. I leave it up to the health professionals to talk about nutrition and the wonderful world of carbohydrates and fats. This book is not about depriving yourself or having to do calculations. It's about good eating habits. Let's opt for the basic principles that appeal to our common sense. Not too much fat. Not too much sugar. And as few processed foods as possible.

The Pantry

Everyone has their own particular tendencies and their favorite food products. There are foods that can serve in a pinch in any situation. I like to keep these in stock: pine nuts, almonds, sesame seeds, canned Italian tomatoes, legumes, pasta, vegetable bouillon, olive oil, onions, garlic, carrots and tofu — these are what I call miracle ingredients (see also page 12).

Improvise

The desire to cook develops with time and practice, as do confidence and instinct. As you go through these recipes, I hope you'll have the desire to modify them, expand on them and add your personal touch, to make this your own cookbook.

Using These Recipes

For success with the recipes, keep these assumptions about what is standard when it comes to basic ingredients; these distinctions are detailed below. For the best results, always use the recommended ingredient, exactly as called for, unless other options are indicated in a tip.

- All eggs used are large eggs.
- Use 2% milk and yogurt unless otherwise specified.
- Butter is salted unless otherwise specified.
- Fresh vegetables and fruits are medium-size unless otherwise indicated. Any inedible peels, skins, seeds and cores are removed unless otherwise indicated.
- "Onions" means regular cooking onions unless otherwise indicated.
- "Mushrooms" means white button mushrooms unless otherwise indicated.
- With canned tomatoes and tomato products, the juice is also used unless the recipe instructs you to drain it.
- Chopped or minced garlic is freshly chopped or minced, not purchased already minced and preserved.
- When greasing barbecue grill, spray with nonstick cooking spray before preheating.

Vegetarian Gourmet Pantry Essentials

By stocking your pantry, refrigerator and freezer with some basics, you can be ready to create terrific meals with ingredients you have on hand in no time at all.

Beans and Legumes • Canned and dried beans, lentils and chickpeas are a terrific base for many meals. Keep a variety of both on hand. Always drain and rinse canned beans or legumes before using. If you don't use the whole can (or you cook extra), store them in an airtight container for up to 2 days or freeze for up to 3 months.

Cheese • If you eat dairy, cheese is an easy way to add a punch of flavor and protein to your meals. Once you open the packaging, rewrap cheeses in clean wrapping and store in the cheese keeper in the refrigerator. It's better to buy smaller amounts more often for the freshest flavor.

Couscous • This is one of the fastest grain products to prepare. Keep it on hand for salads, stuffings and side dishes. Choose whole wheat couscous for extra nutrition.

Nuts • A flavorful source of protein, nuts can be added to all types of recipes from appetizers to desserts. Keep a selection on hand: almonds, walnuts, pecans, pine nuts and any other favorites. Always check that nuts are fresh, purchasing from a source with a high turnover and choosing domestically produced nuts whenever possible. For optimal freshness, store nuts tightly sealed in the freezer for up to 1 year.

Oil • Choose whichever type of mild-flavored vegetable oil you prefer for recipes that use the oil for sautéing. It's best to save any strong-flavored, extra virgin olive oil or nut oils (other than peanut) for salads, dips and other cold foods, or for drizzling on finished dishes rather than for cooking. When cooked, you lose the olive or nut flavor. As well, olive oil tends to burn more easily than other vegetable oils. Store oils in a cool, dark place and check frequently to make sure they smell fresh. You may want to store extra virgin olive oils, nut oils and other ones you use less often in the refrigerator. Let them warm to room temperature for about 15 minutes before using.

Rice • There are many rice varieties available, each with their own distinct flavor and texture. Keep a selection on hand such as basmati, jasmine, Arborio or other short-grain and long-grain rice. Choose brown varieties whenever possible for maximum nutrition. They do take longer to cook, so plan ahead. You can store cooked rice in an airtight container in the refrigerator for up to 2 days or freeze for up to 3 months.

Tamari • A sauce made from soybeans, it is thicker and richer in flavor than soy sauce and is a great way to boost flavor and add a golden brown color to many vegetarian dishes. To keep the sodium level in check, look for sodium-reduced versions. If you don't have tamari, sodium-reduced soy sauce can be substituted in addition to a pinch of sugar or drop of honey.

Tofu • This essential ingredient is an easy source of protein in the vegetarian kitchen. Silken tofu is perfect for recipes when you want to add a thick, creamy texture. It can be puréed into smoothies, sauces and desserts. The block-style tofu comes in different textures: medium, firm and extra-firm. You can often interchange firm and extra-firm in recipes according to your own preference.

Tomatoes • Keep cans of Italian tomatoes, diced, whole and puréed or crushed (ground) to use as a base for sauces, stews and soups. They are far less expensive and more flavorful than tomatoes out of season and require no preparation. If you open a can and don't need all of the tomatoes at once, transfer the extras to an airtight container and refrigerate for up to 3 days or freeze for up to 6 months.

Vegetable Broth • Vegetable broth is essential for soups, stews and sauces. If you don't have time to make it from scratch, the ready-to-use broth in Tetra Paks is a convenient alternative. The flavor varies by brand so do some experimenting and try out different brands until you find the one you like best. Do check the nutrition panels to choose one that is lowest in sodium.

Vinegars • Flavorful vinegars are an easy way to add variety to your meals. Keep a supply of white wine vinegar, red wine vinegar, rice vinegar, balsamic vinegar and cider vinegar on hand. Herb-infused vinegars are an easy way to add a punch of extra flavor.

Whole Grains • Keep dried grains such as quinoa, millet, barley and wheat berries on hand to add oomph to your side dishes, salads and main courses. For extended storage (longer than a few weeks), store whole grains in airtight containers in the freezer. Whole barley and wheat kernels do require almost 1 hour to cook, so cook large batches and freeze the extra in airtight containers for up to 3 months.

Wild Rice • Not a rice at all but the seed of a grass, wild rice is hearty and filling and a nice addition to main courses and side dishes. It does take some time to cook, so make extra and freeze it in an airtight container for up to 3 months so you have it at the ready for last-minute meals.

Measuring Essentials

Liquid Ingredients • For volumes of ¼ cup (60 mL) or more, measure liquid ingredients in a liquid measuring cup — the style with a handle, spout and graduated markings — and be sure to look at eye level to check the measurement accurately. For volumes of less than ¼ cup (60 mL), use measuring spoons.

Dry Ingredients • For volumes of ¼ cup (60 mL) or more, measure dry ingredients in the nesting-style measuring cups that are generally marked with individual sizes: ¼ cup (60 mL), ⅓ cup (75 mL), ½ cup (125 mL), ¾ cup (175 mL) and 1 cup (250 mL). Spoon the ingredient into the cup until it's overflowing, then use a knife or other straightedge to level it off with the top of the cup. Do not pack down or shake the ingredient in the cup. This will allow too much ingredient in the cup and can adversely affect the recipe. For volumes of less than ¼ cup (60 mL), use measuring spoons.

Measuring Prepared Ingredients • When an ingredient is called for as a prepared amount, e.g. ½ cup (125 mL) sliced strawberries, slice the strawberries then measure the volume. If the ingredient is called for whole, then the preparation is specified, e.g. ½ cup (125 mL) strawberries, sliced, so measure whole strawberries then slice them.

Non-specific Amounts for Produce • When produce is called for by a number rather than a volume or weight, this generally means the exact amount isn't crucial to the success of the recipe. It does generally imply medium-size produce unless another size is specified. If you have particularly large or small produce, you may want to add a little less, or more, to the recipe.

Vegetable Roll-Ups

Appetizers

When stomachs start to growl, it's time to move into action. Here's a selection of appetizers and light hors d'oeuvres you can mostly prepare ahead of time. None of them are too filling, so you'll still have room for the events to follow.

Cherry Tomatoes with Cheese 18

Quesadillas 19

Guacamole 20

Cilantro Salsa 21

Hummus 22

Toasted Pita Chips 23

Brie Baguette Bites 24

Parmesan Baguette Bites 25

Bruschetta Baguette Bites 26

Onion Baguette Bites 27

Baked Camembert 28

Polenta Cakes 29

Tofu Cakes 30

Bean Dip 31

Curry Dip 32

Fava Bean Dip 33

Orange Pepper Dip 34

Mushroom Bites 35

Goat Cheese Bites 36

Feta Cheese Bites 37

Vegetable Roll-Ups 38

Mini Pitas with Eggs 39

Cherry Tomatoes with Cheese

Finger food without messy fingers, each tomato is an hors d'oeuvre.

Makes 25

Tip
Pine nuts are the seeds of pinecones. They are fantastic nuts that become more flavorful once they are toasted.

2 tbsp	pine nuts	30 mL
25	cherry tomatoes	25
½ cup	cream cheese, softened	125 mL
	Fresh parsley sprigs	

1. In a dry skillet over medium heat, toast pine nuts, stirring constantly, for 2 to 3 minutes or until golden and fragrant.

2. Cut tops off cherry tomatoes. Remove seeds with a small spoon.

3. In a bowl, mash together cream cheese and pine nuts. Fill tomatoes with cream cheese mixture and place on a serving platter. Garnish with a few sprigs of parsley for color.

Variation

Cherry Tomatoes with Zesty Cheese: Mash ¼ tsp (1 mL) smoked paprika and 1 tsp (5 mL) grated lemon zest into cream cheese before adding pine nuts.

Quesadillas

Fresh basil leaves add an explosion of flavor to these quesadillas, in a perfect recipe for the end of summer.

Serves 4 to 6

¼ cup	creamy goat cheese	60 mL
3	large or small flour tortillas	3
	Olive oil	
1	zucchini, thinly sliced into rounds	1
3	plum (Roma) tomatoes, sliced	3
¼ cup	chopped onion	60 mL
15	basil leaves	15
½ cup	shredded Cheddar cheese	125 mL

1. Spread goat cheese on half of each tortilla.

2. In a skillet, heat 1 tsp (5 mL) oil over medium-high heat. Gently fry zucchini rounds, turning once, until tender.

3. Place zucchini, tomatoes, onion, basil and Cheddar cheese on top of goat cheese. Fold tortillas in half.

4. In a skillet, heat 1 tsp (5 mL) oil over medium heat. Fry one quesadilla, turning once, for 2 to 3 minutes per side until cheese is melted and tortilla is crispy. Repeat with remaining quesadillas, adding more oil between batches as necessary. Cut each quesadilla into two wedges.

Guacamole

You'll love the texture of this dip. Serve with crispy nachos.

Serves 4

Tip

If you like a touch of heat in your guacamole, add hot pepper sauce or a small amount of minced jalapeño pepper.

- **Food processor, optional**

2	very ripe avocados	2
2 tbsp	freshly squeezed lemon juice	30 mL
2 tsp	olive oil	10 mL
1	tomato, seeded and diced	1
1	clove garlic, minced	1
Pinch	granulated sugar	Pinch
	Salt and freshly ground black pepper	

1. In a food processor, purée avocados until smooth. Or use a fork to mash avocados.

2. Stir in lemon juice, olive oil, tomato, garlic, sugar, and salt and pepper to taste. Serve immediately because avocados have a tendency to blacken quickly.

Cilantro Salsa

This recipe can easily be doubled, tripled or even quadrupled, to suit the number of your guests. You'll soon see the bottom of the bowl.

Makes about 1½ cups (375 mL)

Tips

Cilantro is the magic ingredient in this recipe so don't be tempted to leave it out or substitute another herb.

The salsa can be made up to 4 hours ahead of serving. Cover and let stand at room temperature — do not refrigerate it or the tomato will lose its flavor.

1	tomato, diced	1
¼ cup	diced red onion	60 mL
¼ cup	chopped fresh cilantro	60 mL
¼ cup	tomato juice	60 mL
1	chile pepper, chopped	1
	Salt and freshly ground black pepper	

1. In a bowl, combine tomato, red onion, cilantro, tomato juice and chile pepper. Season with salt and pepper to taste.

Variation

Cilantro Avocado Salsa: Add 1 diced avocado with the tomato.

Hummus

Using canned chickpeas means you can prepare this hummus in just a few minutes and no cooking is required. Serve with Toasted Pita Chips (right) or vegetables.

Makes about 1¹/₂ cups (375 mL)

Tips

This recipe can be made lighter by replacing 1 tbsp (15 mL) olive oil with the same amount of water. It's just as tasty.

For presentation, drizzle a little olive oil on top and sprinkle with fresh parsley.

- **Food processor**

1¹/₂ cups	drained rinsed canned chickpeas	375 mL
1	clove garlic, coarsely chopped	1
3 tbsp	freshly squeezed lemon juice	45 mL
1 tbsp	olive oil	15 mL
1 tbsp	tahini	15 mL
¹/₂ tsp	salt	2 mL
	Freshly ground black pepper	

1. In a food processor, purée chickpeas, garlic, lemon juice, olive oil, 3 tbsp (45 mL) water, tahini, salt, and pepper to taste, until smooth and creamy.

Variation

Fresh Herb Hummus: Add 2 tbsp (30 mL) fresh Italian flat-leaf parsley leaves, 6 fresh basil leaves and 2 tsp (10 mL) thyme leaves with the chickpeas.

Toasted Pita Chips

This recipe can be served anytime and anywhere. The toasted pita points are a marvelous accompaniment to hummus, guacamole and dips.

Serves 4

- **Preheat oven to 400°F (200°C)**
- **Baking sheet, lined with parchment paper**

4	pitas	4
	Olive oil	
	Ground cumin	
	Paprika	

1. Cut pitas into points. Place on prepared baking sheet. Brush with olive oil. Sprinkle with cumin and paprika to taste.

2. Bake in preheated oven for about 10 minutes or until bread is crispy. Let cool on pan on a wire rack.

Variation

Replace the cumin and paprika with smoked paprika or your favorite dried herb for a different flavor.

Brie Baguette Bites

The sweet taste of these little hors d'oeuvres will surprise your taste buds.

Makes 12

- **Preheat oven to 350°F (180°C)**
- **Baking sheet, lined with parchment paper**

12	pecan halves	12
12	½-inch (1 cm) slices baguette	12
	Dijon mustard	
12	slices Brie cheese	12
	Pure maple syrup	

1. In a dry skillet over medium heat, toast pecans, stirring constantly, for about 5 minutes or until golden and fragrant. Remove from heat.

2. Place baguette slices on prepared baking sheet. Spread Dijon mustard to taste over one side of each slice. Top each with a slice of Brie and a toasted pecan.

3. Drizzle a little maple syrup over top. Bake in preheated oven for about 1 minute or until cheese is melted.

Variation

For a bolder flavor, replace the pecans with chopped hazelnuts and the Brie with blue cheese, such as Cambozola.

Parmesan Baguette Bites

Here is a simple recipe for a cheese appetizer that can easily accompany a salad.

Makes 12

- **Preheat oven to 350°F (180°C)**
- **Baking sheet, lined with parchment paper**

⅓ cup	cream cheese, softened	75 mL
⅓ cup	chopped fresh parsley	75 mL
2 tbsp	freshly grated Parmesan cheese	30 mL
12	½-inch (1 cm) slices baguette	12

1. In a bowl, combine cream cheese, parsley and Parmesan. Spread mixture evenly on each baguette slice.

2. Place baguette slices on prepared baking sheet. Bake in preheated oven for about 5 minutes or until cheese is warmed.

Variation

Replace the parsley with basil and the Parmesan with Romano cheese.

Bruschetta Baguette Bites

For this cheesy version of a great classic, choose a large clove of garlic. In season, use fresh herbs to add even more flavor to this appetizer.

Makes 12

Tip
Treat your tomatoes with care. The flavor of tomatoes is destroyed by cold temperatures, so never refrigerate them. Store them in a basket at room temperature away from direct sunlight. They're ripe and flavorful when the flesh yields to gentle pressure when squeezed.

- **Preheat oven to 350°F (180°C)**
- **Baking sheet, lined with parchment paper**

2	tomatoes, seeded and diced (see Tip, left)	2
1/4 cup	chopped red onion	60 mL
1	clove garlic, minced	1
1 tsp	dried basil	5 mL
1 tsp	dried parsley	5 mL
2 tsp	olive oil	10 mL
12	1/2-inch (1 cm) slices baguette	12
1 cup	grated sharp (aged) Cheddar cheese	250 mL
Pinch	paprika	Pinch

1. In a bowl, combine tomatoes, red onion, garlic, basil, parsley and olive oil.

2. Placed baguette slices on prepared baking sheet. Spoon tomato mixture on bread. Sprinkle equally with cheese and paprika.

3. Bake in preheated oven for about 5 minutes or until tomato mixture is warmed. Broil for 1 to 2 minutes or until cheese is melted and golden.

Onion Baguette Bites

Children pounce on these hors d'oeuvres, which earn a perfect score for their slightly sweet flavor.

Makes 12

• Preheat oven to 350°F (180°C)

Tip

Cheddar is a popular cheese in Quebec, but its place of origin is the small village of the same name in southern England. We enjoy different varieties of Cheddar, which range from mild to very sharp.

- **Preheat oven to 350°F (180°C)**
- **Baking sheet, lined with parchment paper**

12	½-inch (1 cm) slices baguette	12
	Mayonnaise	
⅓ cup	finely chopped French shallots	75 mL
¼ cup	shredded sharp (aged) Cheddar cheese	60 mL
	Paprika	

1. Spread one side of each baguette slice with mayonnaise and place on prepared baking sheet.

2. Top equally with shallots and Cheddar cheese. Sprinkle with paprika to decorate.

3. Bake in preheated oven for 5 to 10 minutes or until hot and cheese is melted. Broil for 1 to 2 minutes or until cheese is golden.

Baked Camembert

The secret of this recipe is to heat the cheese just enough so it is softened, but not too soft and not runny. Serve with fresh fruit and bread.

Serves 4

Tip

Always check that nuts are fresh, purchasing from a source with a high turnover and choosing domestically produced nuts whenever possible. For optimal freshness, store nuts tightly sealed in the freezer for up to 1 year.

• **Preheat oven to 300°F (150°C)**

3 tbsp	chopped pecans	45 mL
1 tbsp	Basil Pesto (see page 73) or store-bought	15 mL
1	6 oz (170 g) round Camembert cheese	1

1. In a dry skillet over medium heat, toast pecans, stirring constantly, for about 5 minutes or until golden and fragrant. Remove from heat.

2. Spread pesto on top of cheese. Top with toasted pecans.

3. Wrap cheese in foil, sealing edges tightly. Bake in preheated oven for about 10 minutes or just until soft to the touch. Unwrap and carefully transfer to a serving platter.

Variation

Sun-Dried Tomato Baked Camembert: Replace the pecans with pine nuts and use sun-dried tomato pesto in place of the basil pesto.

Polenta Cakes

These tomato-topped cakes are a nice addition to a platter of canapés on sliced baguette or crackers.

Makes about 30 hors d'oeuvres

Tip

The tomato topping can be prepared up to 4 hours ahead. Cover and let stand at room temperature. Do not refrigerate or the tomatoes will become bland.

- Rimmed baking sheet, lined with parchment paper
- $1\frac{1}{2}$- to 2-inch (4 to 5 cm) cookie cutters

Polenta

1 tsp	salt	5 mL
1 cup	cornmeal	250 mL

Topping

2	tomatoes, seeded and diced	2
$\frac{1}{4}$ cup	chopped Spanish onion	60 mL
1	clove garlic, minced	1
2 tbsp	chopped fresh parsley	30 mL
1 tsp	olive oil	5 mL
1 tsp	balsamic vinegar	5 mL
1 tsp	freshly squeezed lemon juice	5 mL
1 tbsp	olive oil, divided (approx.)	15 mL

1. *Polenta:* In a saucepan, bring 4 cups (1 L) water to boil over high heat. Stir in salt. Gradually pour in cornmeal, stirring constantly. Reduce heat and boil gently, stirring constantly, for 5 to 10 minutes or until cornmeal is soft and mixture is very thick. Spread mixture in a thin layer on prepared baking sheet. Let cool until firm and set.

2. Using cookie cutters, cut polenta into about 30 pieces.

3. *Topping:* In a bowl, combine tomatoes, onion, garlic, parsley, 1 tsp (5 mL) olive oil, balsamic vinegar and lemon juice.

4. In a skillet, heat half of the oil over medium heat. In batches, fry polenta pieces, turning once, for about 2 minutes per side or until crisp and golden. Add more oil and adjust heat between batches as necessary.

5. Place polenta cakes on a serving platter and divide topping equally among cakes.

Tofu Cakes

These small appetizers resemble tiny pizzas. Tofu replaces the crust.

Makes 6 cakes

Tip
The block-style tofu comes in different textures: medium, firm and extra-firm. You can often interchange firm and extra-firm in recipes according to your own preference.

- **Preheat oven to 450°F (230°C)**
- **Baking sheet, greased**

1	package (12 oz/340 g) extra-firm tofu (see Tip, left)	1
3	slices red onion, cut in half	3
1	tomato, diced	1
6	kalamata olives, chopped	6
2 tbsp	creamy goat cheese	30 mL

1. Cut tofu across the long side into 6 slices, each about $\frac{3}{4}$ inch (2 cm) thick.

2. Place tofu slices on prepared baking sheet. Top each with a half slice of onion, diced tomato, olives and goat cheese.

3. Bake in preheated oven for about 15 minutes or until hot and starting to brown.

Variation

Replace the kalamata olives with green olives and the goat cheese with freshly grated Parmesan.

Bean Dip

Here is an easy recipe for dip that isn't too rich, but still has a lot of character. The taste will remind you of certain Asian dressings.

Makes about 2 cups (500 mL)

Tips

To toast sesame seeds: In a small, dry skillet over medium heat, toast sesame seeds, stirring constantly, for 2 to 3 minutes or until golden and fragrant. Immediately transfer to a bowl and let cool.

The dip can be prepared up to 1 day ahead, covered and refrigerated. Let warm to room temperature before serving for the best flavor. Garnish with sesame seeds just before serving.

• **Food processor**

2 cups	drained rinsed canned white kidney, cannellini or white pea (navy) beans	500 mL
1/4 cup	light sour cream	60 mL
2 tsp	sesame oil	10 mL
2 tsp	rice vinegar	10 mL
1/2 tsp	ground coriander	2 mL
1/4 tsp	cumin seeds	1 mL
	Salt and freshly ground black pepper	
1 tsp	sesame seeds, toasted, optional (see Tips, left)	5 mL

1. In a food processor, pulse beans, 1/3 cup (75 mL) water, sour cream, sesame oil, vinegar, coriander and cumin seeds until smooth. Season with salt and pepper to taste.

2. Transfer dip to a serving bowl and sprinkle with sesame seeds for more pronounced flavor or simply as a garnish, if desired.

Curry Dip

Curry adds a special touch to this dip. Serve with vegetables, such as carrots and zucchini, cut into sticks.

Makes about 2 cups (500 mL)

Tip

The dip can be prepared up to 1 day ahead, covered and refrigerated. Let stand at room temperature for 15 minutes before serving for the best flavor.

1 cup	light sour cream	250 mL
½ cup	sweet chili sauce	125 mL
¼ cup	mayonnaise	60 mL
2 tsp	red wine vinegar	10 mL
1 tsp	curry powder	5 mL
	Salt and freshly ground black pepper	
	Crumbled feta cheese, optional	

1. In a large bowl, combine sour cream, chili sauce, mayonnaise, vinegar and curry powder. Season with salt and pepper to taste.

2. Transfer to a serving bowl and garnish with feta cheese, if desired.

Variation

Thai Red Curry Dip: In place of the curry powder, in a small skillet, sauté 1 tsp (1 mL) Thai red curry paste in 2 tsp (10 mL) vegetable oil over medium-low heat for 30 seconds. Transfer to a bowl and let cool before adding remaining ingredients. Replace the red wine vinegar with rice vinegar. If you can find coconut yogurt, use it in place of the sour cream.

Cilantro Salsa (page 21)
and Guacamole (page 20)

Hummus (page 22)
and Toasted Pita Chips (page 23)

Leek and Potato Soup (page 43)
and Squash Soup (page 44)

Julienne Vegetable Soup (page 52)
and Broccoli and Cheddar Soup (page 51)

Gazpacho (page 53)

Tofu Soup (page 55)

Legume Salad (page 58)
and Lentil Salad (page 59)

Asian Salad (page 62)
and Spanish Salad (page 60)

Fava Bean Dip

You can find canned fava beans at the supermarket. Very tasty, they also may be labeled Windsor beans or broad beans.

Makes about 1¹⁄₂ cups (375 mL)

Tip

The dip can be prepared up to 1 day ahead, covered and refrigerated. Let stand at room temperature for 30 minutes before serving for the best flavor. Garnish with green onions just before serving.

• **Food processor**

1 cup	drained rinsed canned fava beans	250 mL
¹⁄₂ cup	mayonnaise	125 mL
2 tbsp	apple cider vinegar	30 mL
Pinch	curry powder	Pinch
	Salt and freshly ground black pepper	
2	green onions, chopped	2

1. In a food processor, purée beans until fairly smooth. Add mayonnaise, vinegar and curry powder and pulse until smooth. Season with salt and pepper to taste.

2. Transfer to a serving bowl and garnish with green onions.

Variation

Chili Black Bean Dip: Change up the flavor by using black beans in place of fava beans and chili powder in place of curry powder.

Orange Pepper Dip

The roasted pepper gives this dip its exquisite flavor.

Makes about 1½ cups (375 mL)

Tips

Native to Mexico, the bell pepper is very versatile. We now eat peppers of all colors. Milder and sweeter than green pepper, sweet orange pepper is easier to digest without its skin.

The dip can be prepared up to 1 day ahead, covered and refrigerated. Let stand at room temperature for 15 minutes before serving for the best flavor.

- **Preheat broiler**
- **Food processor**

1	orange bell pepper (see Tips, left)	1
1 cup	cottage cheese	250 mL
½ cup	crumbled feta cheese	125 mL
½	clove garlic	½
	Salt and freshly ground black pepper	

1. On a baking sheet, roast bell pepper under preheated broiler, turning pepper occasionally, for about 15 minutes or until skin blackens.

2. Transfer pepper to an airtight container or bowl covered with plastic wrap and let cool. Remove skin, core and seeds and discard any accumulated liquid.

3. In a food processor, purée pepper, cottage cheese, feta cheese, garlic, and salt and black pepper to taste until smooth. Transfer to a serving bowl.

Mushroom Bites

These appetizers prove that tofu and mushrooms go together beautifully.

Makes 10 appetizers

10	mushrooms, stems removed	10
2 tsp	olive oil	10 mL
3½ oz	firm tofu, cut into 10 cubes	100 g
1 tsp	tamari	5 mL
1 tbsp	sesame seeds	15 mL
1	clove garlic, finely chopped	1
1 tbsp	freshly squeezed lemon juice	15 mL
	Salt and freshly ground black pepper	

Tip

These are best served as soon as they're made. You can assemble the ingredients ahead of time then just sauté at the last minute.

1. Soak mushrooms in water for about 15 minutes.

2. In a skillet, heat oil over medium–high heat. Fry tofu and tamari, turning to brown all sides, until tofu is golden. Stir in sesame seeds (seeds will stick to tofu). Remove skillet from heat and transfer tofu to a bowl.

3. Drain mushrooms and pat dry. Return skillet to medium–high heat. Sauté garlic, drained mushrooms and lemon juice for about 5 minutes or until mushrooms start to brown. Season with salt and pepper to taste.

4. Place a cube of tofu on top of each mushroom cap. Secure together with a toothpick.

Goat Cheese Bites

For this very simple recipe, use high-quality ingredients to ensure success.

**Makes
12 hors d'oeuvres**

<table>
<tr><td colspan="3">• Preheat broiler</td></tr>
<tr><td>2</td><td>red bell peppers</td><td>2</td></tr>
<tr><td>⅓ cup</td><td>creamy goat cheese</td><td>75 mL</td></tr>
</table>

Tips

The peppers can be roasted up to 3 days ahead, covered and refrigerated after peeling and seeding.

You can assemble the rolls up to 8 hours ahead, cover and refrigerate, then let stand at room temperature for 15 minutes before serving for the best flavor.

1. On a baking sheet, roast bell peppers under preheated broiler, turning pepper occasionally, for about 15 minutes or until skin blackens.

2. Transfer peppers to an airtight container or a bowl covered with plastic wrap and let cool. Remove skin, core and seeds and discard accumulated liquid.

3. Slice each pepper lengthwise into 6 strips. Place a spoonful of goat cheese on each strip and roll up. Secure with a toothpick.

Feta Cheese Bites

A favorite cheese appetizer, this has a charming, salty-sweet flavor. Choose premium feta cheese.

Makes about 12 hors d'oeuvres

Tips

One medium zucchini yields about 6 slices.

Greek cheese made from goat's, sheep's or cow's milk, feta is also sold in half-and-half goat's and cow's milk versions.

- **Baking sheet, greased with olive oil**

1	zucchini, cut lengthwise into 6 thin slices (see Tips, left)	1
12	¾-inch (2 cm) cubes feta cheese	12
24	dried cranberries	24

1. Place zucchini slices on prepared baking sheet. Broil, turning partway, watching carefully so they don't burn, for 10 to 15 minutes or until tender and browned.

2. Transfer zucchini slices to a cutting board and cut each in half crosswise.

3. Place a cube of feta cheese at the end of each piece and roll up. Secure with a toothpick. Place rolls with one flat side down on a platter and top with cranberries.

Vegetable Roll-Ups

Serve these vegetarian roll-ups sushi-style.

Serves 6
as an appetizer

Tips
The vegetables can be prepared up to 1 day ahead, covered and refrigerated separately.

You can assemble the rolls up to 8 hours ahead. Wrap tightly in plastic wrap and refrigerate. Let stand at room temperature for about 30 minutes for the best flavor, then cut into rounds just before serving.

• **Preheat oven to 500°F (260°C)**

4	zucchini	4
	Olive oil	
10	stalks asparagus, trimmed	10
½	red bell pepper, cut into strips	½
1	cucumber	1
¾ cup	Hummus (page 22) or store-bought	175 mL
5	large (9 to 10 inch/23 to 25 cm) flour tortillas	5

1. Cut zucchini lengthwise into thin slices. Place on a baking sheet and toss with a little olive oil. Bake in preheated oven for about 10 minutes or until tender and golden. Let cool.

2. In a steamer basket set in a pot of simmering water, steam asparagus and bell pepper for 2 to 3 minutes or until asparagus starts to turn bright green. Transfer to a plate and let cool.

3. Cut cucumber lengthwise into strips. Trim off seeds.

4. Spread hummus on each tortilla. Lay zucchini slices, side by side, to cover tortillas. Divide asparagus, bell pepper and cucumber equally among tortillas and arrange, side by side, in the opposite direction at one edge of the tortillas.

5. Starting at side closest to asparagus, peppers and cucumber, roll up tightly. Cut into 1½-inch (4 cm) rounds.

Mini Pitas with Eggs

Tofu makes this recipe light. The egg spread can also be used in sandwiches or to garnish celery stalks.

Makes 24

Tips

You can put a weight, such as another baking sheet, on the pitas to prevent them from puffing up or pierce them a couple of times before baking.

The pitas can be baked up to 3 days ahead and stored in a cookie tin at room temperature.

The tofu topping can be prepared up to 8 hours ahead, covered and refrigerated. Spoon on top of pitas just before serving.

- **Preheat oven to 450°F (230°C)**
- **Food processor**

24	mini pitas	24
	Olive oil	
Pinch	ground paprika	Pinch
5 oz	medium or firm tofu	150 g
3	eggs, hard-cooked	3
1 tbsp	plain yogurt	15 mL
1 tbsp	mayonnaise	15 mL
1 tsp	Dijon mustard	5 mL
2 tsp	white wine vinegar	10 mL
2 tsp	freshly squeezed lemon juice	10 mL
2	green onions, chopped	2
5	black olives, chopped	5
2	sweet pickles, chopped	2
1 tsp	salt	5 mL
	Freshly ground black pepper	
	Whole black olives	
	Fresh parsley sprigs	

1. Brush pitas with olive oil and sprinkle with a pinch of paprika. Place pitas on a baking sheet and bake in preheated oven for about 5 minutes or until crispy.

2. In a food processor, purée tofu, eggs, yogurt, mayonnaise, Dijon mustard, vinegar and lemon juice until fairly smooth. Transfer to a bowl and stir in green onions, chopped olives, pickles, salt, and pepper to taste.

3. Spoon a large amount of mixture on each pita and serve. Garnish with whole olives and parsley.

Three-Bean Soup
and Lentil Soup

Soups

There's nothing like a bowl of good hot soup to make you feel you've really come home. Soup warms the soul, stimulates the appetite and sets the tone for a meal. It can also add a little spice to your busy midday. Here is a wonderful selection of soups.

Rice Soup 42

Leek and Potato Soup 43

Squash Soup 44

Onion Soup 45

Mushroom Soup 46

Three-Bean Soup 47

Lentil Soup 48

Corn Soup 49

Carrot and Turnip Soup 50

Broccoli and Cheddar Soup 51

Julienne Vegetable Soup 52

Gazpacho 53

Pea Soup 54

Tofu Soup 55

Rice Soup

This is the ideal soup to savor when you've caught a little cold or the Sunday-night blues. The aroma of the basmati rice is divine.

Serves 4

<table>
<tr><td>1 tbsp</td><td>olive oil</td><td>15 mL</td></tr>
<tr><td>1</td><td>onion, chopped</td><td>1</td></tr>
<tr><td>2</td><td>cloves garlic, chopped</td><td>2</td></tr>
<tr><td>1/2 cup</td><td>basmati rice (see Tip, left)</td><td>125 mL</td></tr>
<tr><td>2</td><td>plum (Roma) tomatoes, sliced</td><td>2</td></tr>
<tr><td>1</td><td>zucchini, sliced</td><td>1</td></tr>
<tr><td>1 cup</td><td>drained rinsed canned fava or broad beans</td><td>250 mL</td></tr>
<tr><td>5 cups</td><td>vegetable broth</td><td>1.25 L</td></tr>
<tr><td>1/2 tsp</td><td>salt</td><td>2 mL</td></tr>
<tr><td>1/4 tsp</td><td>dried oregano</td><td>1 mL</td></tr>
<tr><td></td><td>Freshly ground black pepper</td><td></td></tr>
</table>

Tip

You can also use whole-grain brown basmati rice and increase the cooking time to about 30 minutes.

1. In a large pot, heat oil over medium heat. Sauté onion and garlic for about 7 minutes or until golden.

2. Add basmati rice and stir to coat with oil. Stir in tomatoes, zucchini, beans, vegetable broth, salt, oregano, and pepper to taste. Bring to a boil. Reduce heat and simmer for about 15 minutes or until rice is tender.

Leek and Potato Soup

This great classic brims with personality. You don't even need to add cream to make this soup smooth.

Serves 4

Tip

For the best texture in this soup, choose oblong baking potatoes (russet or Idaho) or an all-purpose potatoes, such as a yellow-fleshed variety, rather than round, waxy new potatoes which can make a soup gluey.

- **Food processor, blender or immersion blender, optional**

2 tbsp	olive oil	30 mL
4 cups	chopped leeks (white portion only)	1 L
1	onion, chopped	1
2	cloves garlic, minced	2
2	potatoes, diced (see Tip, left)	2
5 cups	vegetable broth	1.25 L
2	bay leaves	2
1 tsp	dried parsley	5 mL
1/4 tsp	dried basil	1 mL
1/2 cup	milk	125 mL
	Salt and freshly ground black pepper	

1. In a large pot, heat oil over medium heat. Sauté leeks, onion and garlic for about 15 minutes or until golden.

2. Add potatoes, vegetable broth, bay leaves, parsley and basil and bring to a simmer. Reduce heat and simmer for about 20 minutes or until vegetables are very soft.

3. Remove bay leaves. If desired for a smooth soup, in batches, transfer mixture to food processor (or use an immersion blender in the pot) and purée until smooth. Return to pot, if necessary.

4. Stir in milk and reheat over medium heat, stirring often, until steaming (do not let boil). Season with salt and pepper to taste.

Squash Soup

The choice of squash is crucial in this recipe. Buttercup squash is perfect. Its slightly sweet taste and deep orange color make this an irresistible dish.

Serves 4

Tip

If you can't find a buttercup squash, use half of a medium butternut squash. You can roast both halves of the larger squash, use half in the soup, then purée half and freeze in an airtight container for another time.

- **Preheat oven to 450°F (230°C)**
- **Baking dish**
- **Food processor, blender or immersion blender**

1	buttercup squash (see Tip, left)	1
2 tbsp	olive oil, divided	30 mL
2	cloves garlic, cut in half	2
1	red onion, chopped	1
1	potato, diced	1
½	apple, peeled and chopped	½
4 cups	vegetable broth	1 L
1 tsp	salt	5 mL
½ tsp	curry powder	2 mL
	Freshly ground black pepper	

1. Cut squash in half lengthwise. Remove seeds. Place in baking dish, cut side up, and pour 1 tbsp (15 mL) of the olive oil evenly over squash and add garlic.

2. Bake in preheated oven for about 30 minutes or until soft. Peel squash and mash coarsely, reserving garlic.

3. In a pot, heat remaining oil over medium heat. Sauté red onion for about 7 minutes or until starting to brown. Add roasted squash and garlic, potato, apple, vegetable broth, salt, curry and pepper to taste and bring to a simmer. Reduce heat and simmer for about 20 minutes or until vegetables are soft.

4. In batches, transfer mixture to a food processor (or use an immersion blender in pot) and purée until smooth. Return to pot, if necessary, and reheat over medium heat, stirring often, until steaming.

Onion Soup

Who can resist the comfort of a good onion soup — with its cheesy crust on top and what's hidden underneath?

Serves 2

Tip

Other sweet onions work well in this soup. When they're in season, try Vidalia, Walla Walla, Texas Supersweet, Noonday or Bermuda varieties. You may need two if they're medium-size.

2 tbsp	butter	30 mL
1	large Spanish onion, cut into fine strips (see Tip, left)	1
2	cloves garlic, finely chopped	2
1 tbsp	all-purpose flour	15 mL
3 cups	vegetable broth	750 mL
1/3 cup	white wine	75 mL
1	bay leaf	1
1 tsp	salt	5 mL
1/2 tsp	dried parsley	2 mL
1/4 tsp	dried basil	1 mL
1/2 tsp	Dijon mustard	2 mL
6	slices baguette	6
1/2 cup	shredded Gruyère cheese	125 mL

1. In a large pot, melt butter over medium heat. Sauté onion and garlic for about 10 minutes or until golden.

2. Sprinkle with flour and sauté for 1 minute. Gradually stir in vegetable broth until blended. Stir in white wine, bay leaf, salt, parsley, basil and Dijon mustard and bring to a simmer, stirring often. Reduce heat and simmer for about 20 minutes or until onions are very soft and soup is slightly thickened and flavorful. Discard bay leaf.

3. Meanwhile, preheat broiler. Place baguette slices on a baking sheet and broil for 1 to 2 minutes per side or until toasted.

4. Ladle soup into bowls. Top with slices of baguette and cheese.

5. Place bowls on a clean baking sheet and broil for about 5 minutes or until cheese is melted and starting to brown.

Mushroom Soup

A delight for four diners with discerning palates or for two hungry food lovers. You'll discover all the depth of flavor of the mushrooms.

Serves 2 to 4

1 tbsp	olive oil	15 mL
1	onion, chopped	1
1	clove garlic, minced	1
25	white mushrooms, sliced	25
1 tbsp	all-purpose flour	15 mL
2 cups	vegetable broth	500 mL
1 tsp	salt	5 mL
½ tsp	dried savory	2 mL
	Freshly ground black pepper	
2 cups	milk	500 mL

1. In a large pot, heat olive oil over medium heat. Sauté onion for about 7 minutes or until golden. Add garlic and mushrooms and sauté for a few minutes.

2. Sprinkle with flour and sauté for 1 minute. Gradually stir in vegetable broth, then salt, savory and pepper to taste and bring to a simmer, stirring often. Reduce heat and simmer for about 20 minutes or until soup thickens and mushrooms are tender. Stir in milk and heat, stirring often, until steaming (do not let boil).

Variation

For a deeper mushroom flavor, replace half of the white mushrooms with cremini, shiitake caps or oyster mushrooms or a combination.

Three-Bean Soup

A good substantial soup, this one is packed with proteins. The combination of beans and pasta works wonders.

Serves 4

Tip
Herbes de Provence is a blend of dried herbs usually containing thyme, marjoram, tarragon and parsley, and sometimes lavender flowers and rosemary. Look for it at well-stocked grocery stores near the other dried herbs or at bulk food or specialty spice stores. If you don't have it, substitute one herb or a blend of your favorite dried herbs.

1 tbsp	olive oil	15 mL
1	onion, chopped	1
2	cloves garlic, minced	2
1	potato, diced	1
1	carrot, diced	1
4 cups	vegetable broth	1 L
1	can (14 oz/398 mL) plum (Roma) tomatoes	1
1	can (14 to 19 oz/398 to 540 mL) mixed beans, drained and rinsed	1
⅓ cup	whole wheat elbow macaroni	75 mL
½ cup	chopped fresh parsley	125 mL
½ tsp	salt	2 mL
Pinch	herbes de Provence (see Tip, left)	Pinch
	Freshly ground black pepper	

1. In a large pot, heat oil over medium heat. Sauté onion for about 5 minutes or until softened. Add garlic, potato and carrot and sauté for about 5 minutes or until starting to soften.

2. Add vegetable broth, tomatoes, beans, macaroni, parsley, salt, herbes de Provence, and black pepper to taste and bring to a simmer, stirring often. Reduce heat and simmer for about 20 minutes or until vegetables and pasta are tender.

Lentil Soup

Lentils are amazing. They add flavor to any recipe you prepare, and they cook quickly.

Serves 4

Tip

Puy lentils are tiny, French green lentils and are often found at specialty stores. If you can't find them, use regular dried green or brown lentils and increase the cooking time by 5 to 10 minutes.

1 tbsp	olive oil	15 mL
1	onion, chopped	1
2	cloves garlic, minced	2
1	can (14 oz/398 mL) plum (Roma) tomatoes	1
1	carrot, diced	1
1	potato, diced	1
1 cup	dried Puy lentils, rinsed (see Tip, left)	250 mL
½ tsp	salt	2 mL
¼ tsp	paprika	1 mL
¼ tsp	curry powder	1 mL
Pinch	cayenne pepper	Pinch
Pinch	herbes de Provence	Pinch

1. In a large pot, heat oil over medium heat. Sauté onion and garlic for about 5 minutes or until softened. Add tomatoes and boil, breaking up tomatoes with a spoon, for about 5 minutes or until liquid is slightly reduced.

2. Add carrot, potato, lentils, 4 cups (1 L) water, salt, paprika, curry powder, herbes de Provence and cayenne pepper and bring to a simmer. Reduce heat to low, cover and simmer for about 20 minutes or until vegetables and lentils are tender.

Corn Soup

You'll love the combination of this soup's creamy base with the crunchiness of the carrot and zucchini.

Serves 4

Tip

For the best texture in this soup, choose oblong baking potatoes (russet or Idaho) or an all-purpose potatoes, such as a yellow-fleshed variety, rather than round, waxy new potatoes which can make a soup gluey.

• **Food processor**

1 tbsp	olive oil, divided	15 mL
1	onion, chopped	1
1	clove garlic, chopped	1
1	potato, diced (see Tip, left)	1
3 cups	frozen corn kernels	750 mL
4 cups	vegetable broth	1 L
Pinch	dried thyme	Pinch
1 tsp	salt	5 mL
	Freshly ground black pepper	
1	carrot, finely diced	1
1	zucchini, finely diced	1

1. In a large pot, heat 2 tsp (10 mL) of the oil over medium heat. Sauté onion and garlic for about 7 minutes or until golden.

2. Add potato, corn, broth and thyme and bring to a simmer. Reduce heat and simmer for about 20 minutes or until potatoes are soft.

3. Transfer about half to food processor and purée until smooth. Return purée to pot, if necessary, and reheat, stirring often, until steaming. Stir in salt and season with pepper to taste.

4. Meanwhile, in a skillet, heat remaining oil over medium-high heat. Sauté carrot and zucchini for about 5 minutes or until carrot is tender-crisp and zucchini starts to brown. Stir into corn soup or use as garnish by spooning on top of each serving.

Carrot and Turnip Soup

This soup is quick to prepare and turns out well every time. The kids won't even notice the turnip, and will ask for seconds.

Serves 4

Tip

If you don't have time to make broth from scratch, the ready-to-use broth in Tetra Paks is a convenient alternative. The flavor varies by brand so do some experimenting and try out different brands to find one you like. Check the nutritional panel to choose one that is lowest in sodium.

• **Food processor, blender or immersion blender**

1 tbsp	olive oil	15 mL
1	onion, chopped	1
1	clove garlic, chopped	1
3 cups	sliced carrots	750 mL
1	potato, diced	1
½ cup	diced turnip	125 mL
4 cups	vegetable broth (see Tip, left)	1 L
½ tsp	salt	2 mL
½ tsp	dried basil	2 mL
½ tsp	dried parsley	2 mL
½ tsp	celery powder	2 mL
½ tsp	ground coriander	2 mL
	Freshly ground black pepper	

1. In a large pot, heat oil over medium heat. Sauté onion and garlic for about 5 minutes or until softened. Add carrots, potato and turnip and sauté for about 10 minutes or until starting to soften.

2. Add vegetable broth, salt, basil, parsley, celery powder, coriander and pepper to taste and bring to a boil. Reduce heat and simmer for about 20 minutes or until vegetables are soft.

3. In batches, transfer to food processor (or use immersion blender in pot) and purée until smooth and thick. Return to pot, if necessary, and reheat over medium heat, stirring often, until steaming.

Broccoli and Cheddar Soup

Broccoli and cheese go together so well. This soup is a bouquet of subtle flavors.

Serves 4

• **Food processor, blender or immersion blender**

1 tbsp	olive oil	15 mL
½	onion, chopped	½
1	clove garlic, chopped	1
5 cups	chopped broccoli	1.25 L
1	potato, diced	1
½ cup	diced turnip	125 mL
3 cups	vegetable broth	750 mL
1 tsp	salt	5 mL
	Freshly ground black pepper	
1 cup	milk	250 mL
¾ cup	shredded sharp (aged) Cheddar cheese	175 mL

1. In a large pot, heat oil over medium heat. Sauté onion and garlic for about 5 minutes or until softened.

2. Add broccoli, potato, turnip, vegetable broth, salt and pepper to taste and bring to a simmer. Reduce heat to medium-low, cover and simmer for about 20 minutes or until vegetables are soft.

3. In batches, transfer soup to food processor (or use immersion blender in pot) and purée until smooth. Return to pot, if necessary, and stir in milk. Reheat over medium heat, stirring often, until steaming (do not let boil). Remove from heat and stir in cheese until melted.

Variation

Replace all or half of the broccoli with cauliflower and use Swiss cheese in place of the Cheddar for a bolder flavor.

Julienne Vegetable Soup

Simplicity has never tasted so good. Julienning the vegetables adds an original touch to this soup.

Serves 4

1 tbsp	olive oil	15 mL
½	Spanish onion, chopped	½
2	cloves garlic, minced	2
2 cups	julienned zucchini	500 mL
2	carrots, julienned	2
5	mushrooms, julienned	5
4 cups	vegetable broth	1 L
1 tsp	salt	5 mL
¼ tsp	curry powder	1 mL
1 cup	broken rice vermicelli	250 mL

1. In a large pot, heat oil over medium heat. Sauté onion and garlic for about 7 minutes or until golden. Add zucchini, carrots and mushrooms and sauté for about 8 minutes or until starting to soften.

2. Add broth, salt and curry powder and bring to a simmer. Reduce heat and simmer for about 15 minutes or until vegetables are soft.

3. Add rice vermicelli and simmer, stirring gently, for about 3 minutes or until noodles are tender.

Variation

For a bit of Thai flair and heat, replace the curry powder with 1 tsp (5 mL) yellow, red or green Thai curry paste and garnish each serving with torn fresh cilantro leaves.

Gazpacho

There are so many recipes for gazpacho. Here is one you can make in a few minutes, which has the nice, mildly acidic flavor of vinegar. In a heat wave, serve it with ice cubes, and top it with small cubes of onion, tomato, cucumber, peppers and croutons, anytime.

Serves 4

Tip

Treat your tomatoes with care. The flavor of tomatoes is destroyed by cold temperatures so never refrigerate them. Store them in a basket at room temperature away from direct sunlight. They're ripe and flavorful when the flesh yields to gentle pressure when squeezed.

• **Food processor**

4	slices whole wheat bread, crusts removed	4
6	tomatoes (see Tip, left)	6
1	cucumber	1
2	cloves garlic, coarsely chopped	2
1	green bell pepper, coarsely chopped	1
½ cup	tomato juice	125 mL
¼ cup	olive oil	60 mL
1 tbsp	red wine vinegar	15 mL
	Salt	

1. Soak bread in enough water to cover for 2 to 3 minutes.

2. Plunge tomatoes into a pot of boiling water for 1 minute. Immediately transfer to a bowl of ice water and let stand until chilled. Cut out cores and remove skin and seeds.

3. Peel cucumber and remove seeds.

4. In food processor, purée bread, tomatoes, cucumber, garlic, bell pepper, tomato juice, oil and vinegar until just slightly chunky or further for a thinner soup. Season with salt to taste.

Pea Soup

Perfect for people who love sweet soups, this can be made in no time at all, and cooks up to a vivid shade of green.

Serves 4

Tip

If you don't have time to make broth from scratch, the ready-to-use broth in Tetra Paks is a convenient alternative. The flavor varies by brand so do some experimenting and try out different brands to find one you like. Check the nutritional panel to choose one that is lowest in sodium.

• Food processor, blender or immersion blender

1 tbsp	olive oil	15 mL
1	onion, chopped	1
2	cloves garlic, chopped	2
3 cups	frozen green peas	750 mL
3 cups	vegetable broth (see Tip, left)	750 mL
1 cup	coconut milk	250 mL
1/4 tsp	curry powder	1 mL
1	bay leaf	
	Salt and freshly ground black pepper	

1. In a large pot, heat oil over medium heat. Sauté onion and garlic for about 5 minutes or until softened.

2. Stir in peas, vegetable broth, coconut milk, curry powder, bay leaf, and salt and pepper to taste and bring to a simmer. Reduce heat and simmer for about 15 minutes or until peas are soft.

3. Remove bay leaf. In batches, transfer to food processor (or use immersion blender in pot) and purée until smooth. Return to pot, if necessary, and reheat over medium heat, stirring often, until steaming.

Tofu Soup

The tofu is extraordinary in this soup. It brings all the flavors together.

Serves 4

1 cup	rice vermicelli	250 mL
4 cups	vegetable broth	1 L
½ cup	dried sliced mushrooms	125 mL
8 oz	firm or extra-firm tofu, diced	250 g
½ cup	drained canned water chestnuts	125 mL
5	green onions, thinly sliced	5
3 tbsp	tamari	45 mL
1 tbsp	rice vinegar	15 mL
1 cup	bean sprouts	250 mL
	Freshly ground black pepper	

1. In a large pot of boiling water, cook rice vermicelli for 2 to 3 minutes, until tender, or according to package directions. Drain and set aside.

2. In a large pot, bring vegetable broth to a boil over high heat. Add mushrooms, tofu, water chestnuts, green onions, tamari and rice vinegar. Reduce heat and simmer for about 15 minutes or until mushrooms are soft.

3. Stir in rice vermicelli and bean sprouts. Season with pepper to taste.

Wild Rice Salad,
Couscous Salad and Tabbouleh

Salads

Welcome to a wonderful world of salads. Whether you use a base of pasta, greens, grains, legumes, fruit or vegetables, any of these beautiful salads can be served in any season.

Legume Salad 58

Lentil Salad 59

Spanish Salad 60

Greek Salad 61

Asian Salad 62

Hint of Orange Salad 64

Wild Rice Salad 65

Couscous Salad 66

Tabbouleh 67

Divine Salad 68

Crispy Salad 69

Avocado Salad 70

Hearts of Palm Salad 71

Pasta and Brussels Sprouts
  Salad 72

Pasta Salad with Basil Pesto 73

Russian Salad 74

Warm Potato Salad 75

Mango Salad 76

Bread Salad 77

Spaghetti Squash Salad 78

Mandoline Salad 79

Chicory Salad 80

Blue Cheese Salad 81

Legume Salad

This salad can easily become a complete meal when it's served with fresh bread and cheese. It can also be used to fill tortillas.

Serves 4

Tip

Herbes de Provence is a dried herb mixture from southern France. It most often includes thyme, savory, rosemary, marjoram, sage, lavender, bay leaves and basil, as well as fennel seeds. There are many commercial varieties available.

• **Steamer basket**

1	can (14 to 19 oz/398 to 540 mL) mixed beans, drained and rinsed	1
1	tomato, diced	1
2	green onions, cut into pieces	2
½	red or yellow bell pepper, diced	½
½	zucchini, diced	½
1 cup	halved trimmed green beans	250 mL

Dressing

1 tbsp	white wine vinegar	15 mL
1 tbsp	olive oil	15 mL
1 tsp	Dijon mustard	5 mL
Pinch	herbes de Provence (see Tip, left)	Pinch
	Salt and freshly ground black pepper	

1. In a salad bowl, combine mixed beans, tomato, green onions, bell pepper and zucchini.

2. In a steamer basket set in a pot of boiling water, steam green beans for about 5 minutes or until tender-crisp.

3. *Dressing:* In a small bowl, combine vinegar, oil, mustard, herbes de Provence, and salt and black pepper to taste. Pour over vegetables. Wait at least 15 minutes for flavors to blend before serving.

Lentil Salad

Just a few ingredients create a striking blend of flavors. Once you start eating this, it's hard to stop.

Serves 4 to 6

Tip

Puy lentils come from the Puy region of France and have protected designation-of-origin status. There are almost 900 producers of these green lentils, which are appreciated for their crunchy firmness. They are a tiny lentil and are often found at specialty shops. If you can't find them, use regular green or brown lentils instead.

2 cups	Puy lentils, rinsed (see Tip, left)	500 mL
2	tomatoes, diced	2
1/2	red onion, diced	1/2
1 cup	chopped fresh cilantro	250 mL
3 tbsp	balsamic vinegar	45 mL
1 tbsp	olive oil	15 mL
	Salt and freshly ground black pepper	

1. In a pot of boiling water, cook lentils for about 12 minutes or until they are still slightly crunchy.
2. Rinse lentils and put in a large salad bowl. Add tomatoes, red onion, cilantro, vinegar and oil. Add salt and pepper to taste.

Variation

Chickpea Salad: In place of the lentils, use 3 cups (750 mL) drained rinsed canned or cooked chickpeas and 1/2 cup (125 mL) basil in place of the cilantro. Add 1 cup (250 mL) pearl or mini bocconcini or 1/2 cup (125 mL) crumbled feta cheese, if desired.

Spanish Salad

The classic version of this salad is made with canned tuna. Here is a version that is totally vegetarian. It's very easy to make and just as delicious. The Spanish like to sprinkle on the olive oil and red wine vinegar by feel. You can do the same or use the suggested amounts.

Serves 4

1	romaine lettuce, cut into pieces	1
½	Spanish onion, cut into strips	½
30	green cocktail olives	30
4	hard-boiled eggs, quartered	4
2	tomatoes, quartered	2
3 tbsp	olive oil	45 mL
3 tbsp	red wine vinegar	45 mL
	Salt and freshly ground black pepper	

1. In a salad bowl, combine lettuce, onion, olives, eggs and tomatoes.

2. Sprinkle salad with olive oil and red wine vinegar. Add salt and pepper to taste.

Tip

To hard-boil eggs: Place eggs in a saucepan and add enough cold water to cover by 1 inch (2.5 cm). Bring just to a boil over medium-high heat. Remove from heat, cover and let stand for 15 minutes. Run cold water into the pan until eggs are chilled. Drain and then peel off shells.

Greek Salad

The quality of your ingredients will help you make a fantastic salad.

Serves 4

Tip

The kalamata olive tree is a noble tree that gives us a divine fruit. The Kalamata region of Greece is renowned for its fine, very salty olives, which are soaked in brine for a few months before they are shipped around the world.

4	plum (Roma) tomatoes, diced	4
1	cucumber, diced	1
¼	red onion, diced	¼
1 cup	diced feta cheese	250 mL
15	diced black kalamata olives (see Tip, left)	15

Dressing

2 tbsp	freshly squeezed lemon juice	30 mL
1 tbsp	olive oil	15 mL
¼ tsp	dried basil	1 mL
¼ tsp	dried oregano	1 mL
¼ tsp	dried parsley	1 mL
	Salt and freshly ground black pepper	

1. In a large bowl, combine tomatoes, cucumber, red onion, feta and olives.

2. *Dressing:* In a bowl, combine lemon juice, oil, basil, oregano, parsley, and salt and pepper to taste. Add to salad. Let salad stand for at least 30 minutes to allow flavors to blend before serving.

Asian Salad

The dressing for this salad is simply lovely. It marvelously complements the choice of vegetables.

Serves 4

Tips

Pine nuts are expensive but add a terrific flavor and texture. Make sure they are fresh when you purchase them, and store them in an airtight container in the freezer for optimal freshness. Toast them just before using.

Tamari is a sauce made from soybeans. It is thicker and richer in flavor than soy sauce. To keep the sodium level in check, look for sodium-reduced versions. If you don't have tamari, sodium-reduced soy sauce can be substituted with a pinch of sugar or drop of honey.

• **Steamer basket**

2 tbsp	pine nuts (see Tips, left)	30 mL
1 tsp	sesame seeds	5 mL
1 cup	snow peas, trimmed	250 mL
4 oz	spinach, trimmed	125 g
2 cups	bean sprouts	500 mL
½	zucchini, diced	½
1	tomato, diced	1

Dressing

1 tbsp	tamari (see Tips, left)	15 mL
1 tbsp	freshly squeezed lemon juice	15 mL
1 tbsp	rice wine vinegar	15 mL
1 tsp	olive oil	5 mL
1 tsp	tahini (see Tip, right)	5 mL
1 tsp	sesame oil	5 mL
⅛ tsp	ground ginger	0.5 mL
	Freshly ground back pepper	

1. In a dry skillet over medium heat, toast pine nuts and sesame seeds, stirring occasionally, for 2 to 3 minutes or until fragrant and toasted. Be careful: the sesame seeds have a tendency to jump all over the place.

2. In a steamer basket set in a pot of boiling water, steam snow peas for about 5 minutes or until tender-crisp. Rinse under cold water until chilled. Drain well.

3. In a large bowl, combine spinach, bean sprouts, snow peas, zucchini, tomato, pine nuts and sesame seeds.

4. *Dressing:* In a bowl, combine tamari, lemon juice, vinegar, oil, tahini, sesame oil, ginger, and black pepper to taste. Pour over salad just before serving.

Variation

When sugar snap peas are in season, use them in place of the snow peas and use finely shredded napa or other Chinese cabbage in place of the spinach.

Hint of Orange Salad

If you can't find arugula at your supermarket, you can replace it with a mesclun salad mix.

Serves 4

Tips

Arugula can be very strong, even bitter, depending on its level of maturity. It is a salad green with a lot of flavor.

Do not cut endives or avocado until just before serving to prevent browning.

5 cups	arugula (see Tips, left)	1.25 L
2	endives, cores removed, leaves coarsely chopped	2
1	avocado, cut into strips (see Tips, left)	1
1	orange, cut into sections	1
5	black olives, sliced	5
½ cup	diced cucumber	125 mL
1 tbsp	sesame seeds, toasted	15 mL

Dressing

1 tbsp	freshly squeezed lemon juice	15 mL
1 tsp	tahini	5 mL
½ tsp	white wine vinegar	2 mL
½ tsp	tamari	2 mL
½ tsp	sesame oil	2 mL
Pinch	ground ginger	Pinch
	Salt and freshly ground black pepper	

1. In a salad bowl, combine arugula, endives, avocado, orange sections, olives, cucumber and sesame seeds.

2. *Dressing:* In another bowl, combine lemon juice, tahini, vinegar, tamari, sesame oil, ground ginger, and salt and pepper to taste. Pour over salad.

Hearts of Palm Salad (page 71)

Sunny-Side Up Western Sandwiches (page 89)
and Grilled Vegetable Sandwiches (page 88)

Club Sandwich
(page 97)

Frittata (page 100)

Lentil Ratatouille (page 110)

Tofu Tacos (page 113)

Green Pasta (page114), Blue Pasta (page 115) and Red Pasta (page 116)

Pasta with Goat Cheese (page 117)

Wild Rice Salad

You can easily prepare the wild rice ahead of time, then add the rest of the ingredients a few minutes before serving. Sesame oil is essential in this recipe.

Serves 4

Tip

Balsamic vinegar originated in Modena, Italy. There are many different qualities of balsamic vinegar, and not everyone has the means to buy a small bottle of vinegar that has been aged for 15 years. Choose the one that suits your budget.

1 cup	wild rice, rinsed	250 mL
2 tbsp	pine nuts	30 mL
2 tbsp	slivered almonds	30 mL
2	tomatoes, seeded and diced	2
Dash	sesame oil	Dash
Dash	balsamic vinegar (see Tip, left)	Dash
	Salt and freshly ground black pepper	

1. In a saucepan of boiling salted water, cook wild rice until kernels begin to burst, about 1 hour. Let stand, covered, for 10 minutes. Drain and fluff with a fork.

2. In a dry skillet over medium heat, toast pine nuts and almonds, stirring occasionally, for 2 to 3 minutes or until fragrant and toasted.

3. In a salad bowl, combine wild rice, pine nuts, almonds and tomatoes. Add sesame oil, vinegar, and salt and pepper to taste.

Couscous Salad

The children are crazy about this salad. All of their favorite flavors are assembled in the same dish, and the little grains of couscous pop in the mouth.

Serves 4

Tip

Couscous is one of the fastest grain products to prepare. Keep it on hand for salads, stuffings and side dishes. Choose whole wheat couscous for extra nutrition.

1 cup	couscous (see Tip, left)	250 mL
2	green onions, chopped	2
1	cucumber, seeded and diced	1
½	green bell pepper, diced	½
½ cup	chopped fresh parsley	125 mL
1 cup	tomato juice	250 mL
2 tbsp	freshly squeezed lemon juice	30 mL
2 tbsp	olive oil	30 mL
	Salt and freshly ground black pepper	

1. In a large bowl, combine couscous, green onions, cucumber, bell pepper, parsley, tomato juice, lemon juice, oil, and salt and pepper to taste.

2. Cover and refrigerate until couscous has soaked up the juices and flavors have blended.

Variation

Replace the cucumber with yellow zucchini, the green bell pepper with red bell pepper and add ¼ cup (60 mL) chopped fresh basil.

Tabbouleh

Here is my personal version of a great classic. We like it in its pure state, with lots of lemon juice.

Serves 4

Tip

There are as many ways to spell "bulgur" as there are ways to use it. Bulgur is cracked wheat that has been soaked in water to make it swell and soften. The Lebanese use it in their famous tabbouleh.

• Food processor

½ cup	bulgur	125 mL
6 cups	fresh parsley	1.5 L
2	tomatoes, finely chopped	2
½	onion, finely chopped	½
	Juice of 1 lemon	
2 tbsp	olive oil	30 mL
	Salt and freshly ground black pepper	

1. Place bulgur in a large bowl and cover with boiling water. Set aside for about 40 minutes. Drain.

2. In a food processor, chop parsley. In a salad bowl, combine parsley, bulgur, tomatoes, onion, lemon juice, oil, and salt and pepper to taste.

Divine Salad

Here is a salad that always draws oohs and aahs. Each mouthful is a treasure.

Serves 4

Tips

I like using a mixture of sesame seeds, sunflower seeds, slivered almonds and pine nuts.

For a bolder flavor, replace half of the leaf lettuce with torn baby arugula and use goat's milk Cheddar in place of the feta cheese.

• **Steamer basket**

2 tbsp	nuts (see Tips, left)	30 mL
1 cup	green beans, trimmed	250 mL
1	small head curly leaf lettuce	1
2	green onions, chopped	2
1	tomato, diced	1
½	cucumber, diced	½
8	kalamata olives, cut into pieces	8
¼ cup	cubed feta cheese	60 mL
¼ cup	freshly grated Parmesan cheese	60 mL

Dressing

¼ cup	olive oil	60 mL
2 tsp	Dijon mustard	10 mL
2 tbsp	balsamic vinegar	30 mL
2 tbsp	apple cider vinegar	30 mL
Pinch	herbes de Provence	Pinch
	Salt and freshly ground black pepper	

1. In a dry skillet over medium heat, toast nuts, stirring occasionally, for 2 to 3 minutes or until fragrant and toasted.

2. In a steamer basket set in a pot of boiling water, steam green beans for about 5 minutes or until tender-crisp. Rinse under cold water until chilled. Drain well.

3. In a salad bowl, combine lettuce, green beans, green onions, tomato, cucumber, olives, feta cheese, Parmesan cheese and nuts.

4. *Dressing:* In a bowl, slowly combine oil and mustard, stirring constantly. Blend in balsamic vinegar, cider vinegar, herbes de Provence, and salt and pepper to taste. Gently toss into green bean mixture.

Crispy Salad

You'll discover Parmesan crisps with this salad. They're hard to pass up!

Serves 4

- **Preheat oven to 500°F (260°C)**
- **Baking sheet, lined with parchment paper**

1 cup	freshly grated Parmesan cheese	250 mL
	Paprika	
1 tbsp	sesame seeds	15 mL
1 cup	frozen peas	250 mL
4 oz	spinach	125 g
1 cup	bean sprouts	250 mL
2	green onions, chopped	2

Dressing

4 tsp	olive oil	20 mL
1 tbsp	balsamic vinegar	15 mL
2 tsp	Dijon mustard	10 mL
1 tsp	pure maple syrup	5 mL
½	clove garlic, crushed	½

1. On prepared baking sheet, form about 10 small mounds of fresh Parmesan cheese and sprinkle with paprika. Bake in preheated oven for about 5 minutes or until cheese is golden brown and starting to crisp. Let cool on pan on a wire rack for 1 minute, then carefully transfer with a thin spatula to the rack to cool completely.

2. In a dry skillet over medium heat, toast sesame seeds, stirring occasionally, for 2 to 3 minutes or until fragrant and toasted.

3. In a saucepan of boiling water, steam peas until soft.

4. *Dressing:* Meanwhile, in a bowl, combine oil, vinegar, mustard, maple syrup and garlic.

5. In a salad bowl, combine spinach, peas, bean sprouts, green onions and sesame seeds. Add Parmesan crisps and drizzle with dressing.

Avocado Salad

The avocado gives this salad all its richness, and blends perfectly with the flavor of the grapefruit.

Serves 4

Tip

Radicchio is a very compact red-and-white salad from the chicory family. Radicchio's bitter leaves keep a long time.

• Steamer basket

1	avocado	1
1 tbsp	freshly squeezed lemon juice	15 mL
6	spears asparagus	6
1	pink grapefruit, peeled and sliced	1
2	green onions, chopped	2
1	head radicchio, leaves separated (see Tip, left)	1

Dressing

1 tbsp	olive oil	15 mL
2 tsp	balsamic vinegar	10 mL
1 tsp	liquid honey	5 mL
1 tsp	Dijon mustard	5 mL
½	clove garlic, crushed	½

1. Cut avocado into strips and sprinkle with lemon juice to prevent browning.

2. Trim tough ends from asparagus and discard. In a steamer basket set in a pot of boiling water, steam asparagus for about 5 minutes or until tender–crisp. Rinse under cold water until chilled. Drain well. Cut into pieces.

3. In a salad bowl, combine avocado, grapefruit, green onions, asparagus and radicchio.

4. *Dressing:* In a bowl, combine oil, vinegar, honey, mustard and garlic. Add dressing to vegetables and serve.

Hearts of Palm Salad

Here is an original and delicious salad recipe. The hearts of palm are at their best in the salad.

Serves 4

Tip

Apple cider vinegar has antioxidant properties. It is apple juice that has been aged in oak barrels. It is appreciated for its fruity flavor.

- **Steamer basket**

1	can (14 oz/398 mL) hearts of palm, drained	1
1½ cups	halved green beans	375 mL
2	tomatoes, diced	2
½ cup	black olives, sliced	125 mL
1 tbsp	mayonnaise	15 mL
1 tbsp	apple cider vinegar (see Tip, left)	15 mL
1 tbsp	olive oil	15 mL
	Fresh or dried basil	

1. Cut hearts of palm into rounds and place in a bowl.

2. In a steamer basket set in a pot of boiling water, steam green beans for about 5 minutes or until tender-crisp. Rinse under cold water until chilled. Drain well and add to hearts of palm.

3. In a salad bowl, combine tomatoes, olives, mayonnaise, cider vinegar, olive oil, and basil to taste. Add to bowl with hearts of palm and green beans just before serving.

Pasta and Brussels Sprouts Salad

This salad is a nice way to rediscover Brussels sprouts.

Serves 4

Tip
Use pasta that has visual appeal, such as chifferi or rotini. Chifferi are short, fat, curled tubes, usually ridged and similar to elbow macaroni.

• **Steamer basket**

12 oz	pasta, such as chifferi or rotini (see Tip, left)	375 g
15	Brussels sprouts, trimmed and cut in half lengthwise	15
1	zucchini, diced	1
¼	onion, chopped	¼
1	tomato, seeded and diced	1
1	carrot, grated	1
2 tbsp	mayonnaise	30 mL
1 tbsp	olive oil	15 mL
½ tsp	curry powder	2 mL
Pinch	herbes de Provence (see Tip, page 47)	Pinch
	Salt and freshly ground black pepper	

1. In a pot of boiling salted water, cook pasta for about 10 minutes or according to package directions. Drain and rinse under cold water.

2. In a steamer basket set in a pot of boiling water, steam Brussels sprouts for about 10 minutes or until tender-crisp. Rinse under cold water until chilled. Drain well.

3. In a salad bowl, combine pasta, Brussels sprouts, zucchini, onion, tomato, carrot, mayonnaise, oil, curry powder, herbes de Provence, and salt and pepper to taste.

Pasta Salad with Basil Pesto

Both adults and kids love this simple, mouthwatering salad that's delicious hot or cold.

Serves 4 to 6

Tips

Pesto is a magical mixture — of basil leaves, garlic, olive oil and pine nuts — which originated in Italy. The word "pesto" means "ground." Traditionally, the ingredients were ground in a mortar.

You will not use all the pesto in this recipe. You can freeze the remainder in small plastic containers, each about ½ cup (125 mL), until you need it. I make a large quantity of pesto in the summer, using fresh basil, to supply me for the year.

• **Food processor**

1 lb	penne pasta	500 g

Basil Pesto (see Tips, left)

50	fresh basil leaves	50
10	spinach leaves	10
2	cloves garlic, coarsely chopped	2
¼ cup	pine nuts, toasted	60 mL
¼ cup	freshly grated Parmesan cheese	60 mL
½ tsp	salt	2 mL
	Freshly ground black pepper	
1 cup	extra virgin olive oil	250 mL
½ cup	freshly grated Parmesan cheese	125 mL

1. In a large pot of boiling salted water, cook pasta for about 10 minutes or according to package directions. Drain and rinse in cold water.

2. *Basil Pesto:* Meanwhile, in a food processor, purée basil, spinach, garlic, pine nuts, ¼ cup (60 mL) Parmesan, salt, and pepper to taste. With motor running, slowly add oil through the feed tube until integrated.

3. In a large bowl, combine pasta, 3 tbsp (45 mL) of the pesto and ½ cup (125 mL) Parmesan.

Russian Salad

Here is a new version of Russian salad. The creamy sauce is lightened up with light sour cream.

Serves 4

Tip

To hard-boil eggs: Place eggs in a saucepan and add enough cold water to cover by 1 inch (2.5 cm). Bring just to a boil over medium-high heat. Remove from heat, cover and let stand for 15 minutes. Run cold water into the pan until eggs are chilled. Drain and then peel off shells.

- **Steamer basket**

4	potatoes (each about 6 oz/175 g)	4
1 cup	diced carrots	250 mL
1 cup	frozen peas	250 mL
1 cup	frozen corn kernels	250 mL

Sauce

2 tbsp	light sour cream	30 mL
2 tbsp	mayonnaise	30 mL
2 tbsp	freshly grated Parmesan cheese	30 mL
1 tsp	Dijon mustard	5 mL
2 tsp	vinegar	10 mL
	Salt and freshly ground black pepper	
2	hard-boiled eggs, sliced (see Tip, left)	2
¼ cup	green olives, cut into pieces	60 mL

1. Place potatoes in a pot and add enough cold salted water to cover. Bring to a boil over high heat. Reduce heat and boil gently for about 20 minutes or until potatoes are tender. Drain well and let cool slightly. Peel potatoes and dice (you should have 3 cups/750 mL).

2. In a steamer basket set in a pot of boiling water, steam carrots, peas and corn for about 5 minutes or until tender–crisp.

3. *Sauce:* Meanwhile, in a bowl, combine sour cream, mayonnaise, Parmesan, mustard, vinegar and salt and pepper to taste.

4. In a salad bowl, combine potatoes, carrots, peas, corn, eggs and olives. Add sauce and toss well. Let stand for about 10 minutes for flavors to blend before serving.

Warm Potato Salad

Mustard plays a starring role in this delicious recipe. Do not hesitate to double the recipe.

Serves 2 to 4

1 tbsp	olive oil	15 mL
¼	onion, chopped	¼
1	clove garlic, chopped	1
1	carrot, diced	1
1	potato, diced	1
1 cup	cauliflower, cut into small pieces	250 mL
3 tbsp	mustard, divided	45 mL
1	zucchini, diced	1
1 cup	bean sprouts	250 mL
	Salt and freshly ground black pepper	

1. In a large pot, heat oil over medium heat. Sauté onion and garlic for about 3 minutes or until starting to soften. Add carrot and potato and sauté for about 5 minutes or until carrots start to soften.

2. Add cauliflower and 1 tbsp (15 mL) of the mustard and stir together. Add zucchini and another 1 tbsp (15 mL) of mustard and sauté for 2 to 3 minutes more or until potatoes are still crunchy.

3. Add bean sprouts and remaining 1 tbsp (15 mL) of mustard. Season with salt and pepper to taste.

Variation

For a milder flavor and creamy texture, use 2 tbsp (30 mL) plain yogurt in Step 3 instead of the remaining 1 tbsp (15 mL) mustard.

Mango Salad

The quality of the ingredients is what really makes this salad a success. It's easy to make and juicy to perfection.

Serves 2 to 4

(see Tip, left)

1½ cups	diced ripe mangos	375 mL
1½ cups	diced tomatoes	375 mL
¼	red onion, cut into strips	¼
2 tsp	balsamic vinegar	10 mL
1 tsp	olive oil	5 mL
1 tbsp	chopped fresh cilantro (see Tip, left)	15 mL
	Salt and freshly ground black pepper	

> **Tip**
> Cilantro is an herb with a unique flavor, which is frequently used in Asian cuisine. It is sometimes called Chinese parsley or coriander.

1. In a salad bowl, combine mangos and tomatoes. Add red onion, vinegar, oil, cilantro, and salt and pepper to taste. Mix well. Let stand for about 10 minutes to allow flavors to blend before serving.

Variation

Green Mango Salad: Use green mangos in place of the ripe mangos and replace the tomatoes with 1 large red bell pepper, cut into thin strips. Replace the balsamic vinegar with freshly squeezed lime juice or rice vinegar.

Bread Salad

The idea of a bread salad may seem surprising, but the result is a delight.

Serves 2 to 4

Tip

Treat your tomatoes with care. The flavor of tomatoes is destroyed by cold temperatures so never refrigerate them. Store them in a basket at room temperature away from direct sunlight. They're ripe and flavorful when the flesh yields to gentle pressure when squeezed.

8	slices ($\frac{1}{2}$ inch/1 cm) baguette	8
3	plum (Roma) tomatoes, seeded and diced (see Tip, left)	3
1	cucumber, diced	1
$\frac{1}{4}$	red onion, diced	$\frac{1}{4}$
1	clove garlic, crushed	1
10	fresh basil leaves	10
3 tbsp	white wine vinegar	45 mL
1 tbsp	olive oil	15 mL
	Salt and freshly ground black pepper	

1. Toast baguette slices in the toaster or under broiler. Cut slices into cubes and set aside.

2. In a salad bowl, combine tomatoes, cucumber, red onion, garlic, basil, vinegar, oil, and salt and pepper to taste. Add bread croutons 2 to 3 minutes before serving so they remain crunchy.

Variation

Roasted Red Pepper Bread Salad: Replace 2 of the tomatoes with 1 roasted red bell pepper, chopped, and use 4 cloves of roasted garlic, mashed, in place of the fresh garlic.

Spaghetti Squash Salad

This salad can be prepared with leftover spaghetti squash. You can also cook a squash for the occasion, but the preparation time will be a little longer.

Serves 2 to 4

Tips

If you don't have spaghetti squash, you can use 3 cups (750 mL) roasted cubed butternut or acorn squash on its own or in combination with roasted cubed zucchini.

Herbes de Provence is a blend of dried herbs usually containing thyme, marjoram, tarragon and parsley, and sometimes lavender flowers and rosemary. Look for it at well-stocked grocery stores with the other dried herbs or at bulk food or specialty spice stores. If you don't have it, substitute one or a blend of your favorite dried herbs.

- **Preheat oven to 400°F (200°C)**

1	spaghetti squash (see Tips, left)	1
1 tbsp	olive oil (approx.)	15 mL
½	zucchini, diced	½
1½ cups	sliced mushrooms	375 mL
Pinch	herbes de Provence (see Tips, left)	Pinch
Dash	tamari or soy sauce	Dash
1	plum (Roma) tomato, diced	1
½ cup	crumbled feta cheese	125 mL
5	black olives, diced	5
2	green onions, diced	2
1 tsp	balsamic vinegar	5 mL

1. Cut spaghetti squash in half lengthwise and scoop out seeds. Place on a baking sheet and bake in preheated oven for about 40 minutes or until soft. Use a fork to shred the flesh of the squash. You should have about 4 cups (1 L).

2. In a skillet, heat oil over medium heat. Sauté zucchini and mushrooms for 2 to 3 minutes or until tender. Set aside.

3. In same skillet, add flesh from spaghetti squash, herbes de Provence and tamari and sauté for 2 to 3 minutes or until heated through.

4. In a salad bowl, combine squash mixture, zucchini, mushrooms, tomato, feta, olives and green onions. Add a dash of olive oil and balsamic vinegar. Serve hot or cold.

Mandoline Salad

This one is for lovers of crunchy vegetables. If you do not have a mandoline slicer, you can cut the vegetables into very thin slices with a knife.

Serves 4

2	carrots, thinly sliced	2
1	cucumber, thinly sliced	1
1 cup	thinly sliced cabbage	250 mL
1 cup	alfalfa sprouts	250 mL
3 tbsp	freshly squeezed lemon juice	45 mL
1 tbsp	vinegar	15 mL
1 tbsp	olive oil	15 mL
	Salt and freshly ground black pepper	

Tip

I prefer to pour the vinegar into the mixture before the oil. The vinegar adheres better to un-oiled foods, especially lettuce.

1. In a salad bowl, combine carrots, cucumber and cabbage.

2. Add alfalfa sprouts, lemon juice, vinegar, oil, and salt and pepper to taste.

Variation

Asian Mandoline Salad: Use napa or Chinese cabbage in place of the regular cabbage, bean sprouts in place of the alfalfa sprouts and freshly squeezed lime juice in place of the lemon juice and vinegar. Add 1 tsp (5 mL) liquid honey, or to taste, once the salad is tossed together. If you like heat, add Asian hot chili sauce to taste.

Chicory Salad

Chicory gives this recipe its bitterness and crunch, and contrasts nicely with the sweet flavor of the dressing.

Serves 4

Tip

Frisée, also known as curly chicory and curly endive, has long, slender spiky green leaves. Its bitter leaves are often included in mesclun mix.

• **Steamer basket**

¼ cup	slivered almonds	60 mL
1 cup	sugar snap peas	250 mL
5 cups	frisée (see Tip, left)	1.25 L
⅓ cup	thinly sliced strips red onion	75 mL
1	tomato, diced	1
¼ cup	green olives, cut into pieces	60 mL
¼ cup	freshly grated Parmesan cheese	60 mL

Dressing

¼ cup	olive oil	60 mL
1 tsp	Dijon mustard	5 mL
1 tbsp	apple cider vinegar	15 mL
1½ tsp	balsamic vinegar	7 mL
1	egg yolk, hard-boiled (see Tip, page 74)	1
1 tsp	liquid honey	5 mL
2	sweet pickles, diced	2
Pinch	dried oregano	Pinch
	Salt and freshly ground black pepper	

1. In a dry skillet over medium heat, toast almonds for 2 to 3 minutes or until fragrant and toasted.

2. In a steamer basket set in a pot of boiling water, steam peas for about 5 minutes or until tender-crisp. Rinse under cold water until chilled. Drain well.

3. In a large bowl, combine frisée, red onion, almonds, peas, tomato, olives and Parmesan cheese.

4. *Dressing:* In a bowl, combine oil and mustard. Add cider vinegar, balsamic vinegar, egg yolk, honey, pickles, oregano, and salt and pepper to taste. Add to salad.

Blue Cheese Salad

For people who love blue cheese, this salad is divine.

Serves 4

Tip

Make sure the blue cheese is crumbled into small pieces.

1 tbsp	olive oil	15 mL
½ cup	pecans	125 mL
1	head radicchio, leaves separated (see Tip, page 70)	1
8 oz	spinach	250 g
2	Anjou pears, sliced	2

Dressing

½ cup	crumbled Gorgonzola blue cheese (see Tip, left)	125 mL
¼ cup	olive oil	60 mL
2 tbsp	freshly squeezed lemon juice	30 mL
	Freshly ground black pepper	

1. In a skillet, heat oil over medium heat. Toast pecans for 2 to 3 minutes or until fragrant and toasted.

2. In a salad bowl, combine pecans, radicchio, spinach and pears.

3. *Dressing:* In a bowl, combine blue cheese, oil, lemon juice, and pepper to taste. If there is not enough liquid, add 1 to 2 tbsp (15 to 30 mL) of water or until desired consistency. Pour dressing over salad before serving.

Chickpea Stew

Main Dishes

Vegetarian mains are surprisingly versatile and varied. From omelets to stews to pasta, here is a feast of quick and tasty foods.

Hearty Minestrone 84

Risotto with Sun-Dried Tomatoes . . . 85

Lentil Pie 86

Onion Pie 87

Grilled Vegetable Sandwiches 88

Sunny-Side Up Western
   Sandwiches 89

Rice Quiche 90

Spinach Quiche 92

Tofu Pita Sandwiches 93

Bagel Melt 94

Cauliflower Omelet 95

Three-Bean Omelet 96

Club Sandwich 97

Stuffed Tomato with Egg 98

Hard-Boiled Eggs with Lentils 99

Frittata 100

All-Dressed Pizza 101

Four-Cheese Pizza 102

Pesto Pizza 103

Burritos 104

Chickpea Stew 105

Mini Lasagnas 106

Creamy Lentils 108

Lentils with Cumin 109

Lentil Ratatouille 110

Chili sin Carne 111

Spaghetti Sauce 112

Tofu Tacos 113

Green Pasta 114

Blue Pasta 115

Red Pasta 116

Pasta with Goat Cheese 117

Macaroni with Tomato
   and Cheese 118

Pecan Paradise Pasta 119

Couscous with Prunes 120

Spinach Ricotta Cannelloni 122

Curry Couscous 124

Tofu with Peanut Sauce 125

Tofu Brochettes 126

Vegetable Stir-Fry 127

Vegetable Curry 128

Veggie Burger 129

Cheese Fondue 130

Sweet Potato Shepherd's Pie 131

Polenta Mountain 132

Vegetarian Chop Suey 134

Vegetable Paella 135

Stuffed Squash 136

Stuffed Peppers 137

Hearty Minestrone

The family will squabble over who gets the cabbage leaves. This soup is so substantial it can easily serve as a meal, accompanied by good bread.

Serves 4

Tip
You can serve the soup "wrapped" in a cabbage leaf. Using tongs, remove cabbage leaves from soup and line each bowl, then ladle soup on top.

1 tbsp	olive oil	15 mL
1	onion, diced	1
1	clove garlic, chopped	1
1 cup	diced carrots	250 mL
1 cup	diced potatoes	250 mL
1 cup	diced zucchini	250 mL
1/2 cup	diced celery	125 mL
2	tomatoes, diced	2
5 cups	vegetable broth	1.25 L
1 cup	drained rinsed canned kidney beans	250 mL
1 tsp	salt	5 mL
1/8 tsp	dried thyme	0.5 mL
1	bay leaf	1
4	leaves Savoy cabbage, cut in half	4
1/2 cup	freshly grated Parmesan cheese	125 mL
	Freshly ground black pepper	

1. In a large pot, heat oil over medium heat. Sauté onion and garlic for about 5 minutes or until softened. Add carrots, potatoes, zucchini and celery and sauté for 8 minutes or until starting to soften.

2. Stir in tomatoes, broth, beans, salt, thyme and bay leaf and bring to a simmer. Lay cabbage leaves on top and cover pot with lid. Simmer for about 20 minutes or until vegetables are soft and soup is flavorful. Stir in Parmesan and season with pepper to taste. Discard bay leaf.

Risotto with Sun-Dried Tomatoes

For a little comfort food on the side, stir up this rich, creamy risotto.

Serves 4

Tips

A specialty of
northern Italy, risotto
is renowned for its
simplicity and its
slightly smooth yet
chewy texture.
Short-grain, high-starch
Arborio rice is the
traditional choice for
this classic dish, and
gives it a distinctive
creaminess.

To toast pine nuts: In a
small, dry skillet over
medium heat, toast pine
nuts, stirring constantly,
for about 3 minutes
or until golden and
fragrant. Immediately
transfer to a bowl and
let cool.

3 cups	vegetable broth	750 mL
1 tbsp	olive oil	15 mL
2	cloves garlic, minced	2
1	onion, chopped	1
1 cup	Arborio rice (see Tips, left)	250 mL
5	oil-packed sun-dried tomatoes, drained and cut into pieces	5
½ cup	frozen green peas	125 mL
2 tbsp	pine nuts, toasted (see Tips, left)	30 mL
½ cup	freshly grated Parmesan cheese	125 mL

1. In a saucepan, heat vegetable broth over high heat until simmering. Reduce heat to low, cover and keep hot.

2. In a skillet, heat oil over medium–high heat. Sauté garlic and onion for about 5 minutes or until golden. Add rice and sauté for 1 minute until well coated. Reduce heat to medium.

3. Stir in 1 cup (250 mL) of the broth and simmer, stirring often, until liquid is absorbed. Gradually add more broth, about ⅓ cup (75 mL) at a time, and continue to simmer, stirring often. Wait until broth is completely absorbed before adding more broth. When you have added two-thirds of the broth, stir in sun-dried tomatoes and peas. Cook, gradually adding broth until rice is tender but firm. At the end of cooking, stir in pine nuts and Parmesan cheese. Serve immediately.

Lentil Pie

You'll be amazed how well this hearty pie holds together.

Serves 4

• Preheat oven to 350°F (180°C)

1	baked 9-inch (23 cm) pie crust	1
1 tbsp	olive oil	15 mL
1	onion, chopped	1
1	clove garlic, chopped	1
1	carrot, diced	1
1	stalk celery, diced	1
2 cups	drained rinsed canned or cooked brown or green lentils (see Tip, left)	500 mL
1	can (14 oz/398 mL) plum (Roma) tomatoes	1
2 tbsp	sesame seeds	30 mL
2 tbsp	drained capers	30 mL
$\frac{1}{2}$ tsp	dried savory	2 mL
$\frac{3}{4}$ cup	shredded sharp (aged) Cheddar cheese	175 mL

Tip

One 19-oz (540 mL) can lentils will yield 2 cups (500 mL) drained and rinsed. If you have smaller cans, use two and measure out the amount needed for the recipe. Extra lentils can be refrigerated in an airtight container for up to 2 days or frozen for up to 3 months. To cook from dried, rinse and cook 1 cup (250 mL) dried lentils.

1. In a skillet, heat oil over medium heat. Sauté onion and garlic for 5 minutes or until softened.

2. Stir in carrot, celery, lentils, tomatoes, sesame seeds, capers and savory and bring to a boil. Boil gently, stirring occasionally and breaking up tomatoes with a spoon, until thick. Spoon mixture into pie crust. Sprinkle cheese on top.

3. Bake in preheated oven for about 20 minutes or until filling is hot and cheese is melted. Let cool for 10 minutes before cutting into 8 wedges.

Onion Pie

A pie with a very refined taste, this one's best beside a well-dressed green salad.

Serves 4

Tip

You can use other varieties of sweet onion in place of the Spanish onion. Try Vidalia, Walla Walla or other sweet varieties when they're in season.

• **Preheat oven to 350°F (180°C)**

1	baked 9-inch (23 cm) pie crust	1
1 tbsp	Dijon mustard	15 mL
1 tbsp	olive oil	15 mL
1	Spanish onion, cut in half lengthwise and cut into thin strips (see Tip, left)	1
1	clove garlic, chopped	1
1	tomato, sliced	1
¾ cup	shredded Swiss cheese	175 mL

1. Brush inside of pie crust with Dijon mustard.

2. In a skillet, heat oil over medium–high heat. Sauté onion and garlic for about 10 minutes or until softened and slightly caramelized. Spoon into pie crust.

3. Arrange tomato slices on top and sprinkle with cheese. Bake in preheated oven for about 20 minutes or until filling is hot. Broil for about 3 minutes or until cheese is browned. Let stand for 10 minutes before cutting into 8 wedges.

Grilled Vegetable Sandwiches

This sandwich is stuffed with a lot of character.

Serves 2

□

Tip

The zucchini, onion and mushrooms can be cooked ahead, cooled, covered and refrigerated for up to 2 days. Serve cold or reheat before building sandwiches.

- **Preheat broiler**
- **Rimmed baking sheet, brushed with olive oil**

2	zucchini	2
2	slices red onion	2
1½ tbsp	olive oil, divided	22 mL
6	mushrooms, sliced	6
	Dijon mustard	
2	kaiser rolls, split	2
¼ cup	creamy goat cheese	60 mL
	Alfalfa sprouts	
1	tomato, sliced	1

1. Cut zucchini lengthwise into thin slices. Place on prepared baking sheet with red onion slices. Brush with 1 tbsp (15 mL) of the oil. Broil, turning once, for 4 to 5 minutes per side or until tender and browned. Watch carefully to ensure they don't burn.

2. In a small skillet, heat remaining oil over medium-high heat. Sauté mushrooms for about 5 minutes or until liquid is released and mushrooms are browned.

3. Spread Dijon mustard to taste on cut sides of rolls, then spread with goat cheese. Divide zucchini, red onions and mushrooms equally on bottom halves and top with alfalfa sprouts and tomato slices. Sandwich with tops.

Sunny-Side Up Western Sandwiches

Whenever I was pregnant, I could easily have gobbled up more than one of these sandwiches. Purists who have a horror of processed cheese slices can opt for Cheddar cheese, instead.

Serves 2

Tip
Always crack eggs individually into a small bowl before adding to a pan or a batter to avoid getting pieces of shell or a bad egg mixed in with other ingredients.

• **Preheat oven to 300°F (150°C)**

2	pieces (each 4 inches/10 cm) baguette	2
	Dijon mustard	
2 cups	mesclun salad mix	500 mL
1	tomato, sliced	1
2	thin slices red onion, cut in half	2
2	slices processed cheese	2
1 tsp	vegetable oil	5 mL
2	eggs	2

1. Cut baguette pieces in half lengthwise. Scoop out the soft part. In each piece spread Dijon mustard, then arrange mesclun mix, red onions and a slice of cheese on bottom halves. Place both halves on a baking sheet and bake in preheated oven for 3 minutes or until warmed.

2. Meanwhile, in a large skillet, heat oil over medium heat. Add eggs and fry, sunny-side up, until golden around the edges and whites are set. Place 1 egg in each sandwich. The first bite will break the egg yolk and make your sandwich runny.

Rice Quiche

Here's an appealing alternative for those who are not so fond of flaky pie crust.

Serves 4 to 6

Tip

If you prefer, you can cook the rice in the microwave or a rice cooker instead of on the stovetop. Follow package directions or your microwave or rice cooker instruction manual.

- **Preheat oven to 350°F (180°C)**
- **9-inch (23 cm) glass pie plate, greased**

Crust

1 cup	basmati rice, rinsed (see Tip, right)	250 mL
2 cups	water	500 mL
1 tsp	butter	5 mL
1	egg	1

Filling

2 tbsp	butter	30 mL
2 tbsp	all-purpose flour	30 mL
1 cup	milk	250 mL
1 tbsp	olive oil	15 mL
1	onion, chopped	1
1	clove garlic, chopped	1
1	zucchini, diced	1
4 oz	sliced mushrooms	125 g
1 cup	chopped broccoli	250 mL
½ tsp	salt	2 mL
	Freshly ground black pepper	
6	asparagus tips	6
¾ cup	shredded sharp (aged) Cheddar cheese	175 mL

1. *Crust:* In a saucepan, combine rice, water and butter and bring to a boil over high heat. Reduce heat to low, cover and simmer for 15 minutes or until rice is tender and liquid has been absorbed. Let stand, covered, for 5 minutes. Fluffy with a fork, transfer to a bowl and let cool. Stir in egg until blended. Press into prepared pie plate to form a crust.

2. *Filling:* In a small saucepan, melt butter over medium heat. Sprinkle with flour and cook, stirring, for 1 minute. Gradually whisk in milk. Bring to a simmer, whisking constantly. Reduce heat and simmer, stirring, for about 3 minutes or until sauce is thick. Remove from heat.

Tip
Basmati is a
long-grain rice grown
in the foothills of the
Himalayas. It is famous
for its fragrance, hence
its name. Basmati is
Hindi for "queen of
fragrance."

3. In a large skillet, heat oil over medium heat. Sauté onion, garlic, zucchini, mushrooms and broccoli for about 8 minutes or until tender-crisp. Transfer to a bowl. Stir in salt, and pepper to taste. Set aside.

4. In a steamer basket or a small saucepan with a small amount of boiling water, steam asparagus tips for about 2 minutes or until they turn bright green. Drain.

5. Stir onion mixture into sauce until coated and spoon into pie shell. Sprinkle Cheddar cheese on top, then arrange asparagus tips on top. Bake in preheated oven for about 20 minutes.

Variation

If asparagus isn't in season, substitute green beans for the asparagus or use 12 halved cherry or grape tomatoes, skip Step 4 and arrange, cut side up, on top of cheese.

Spinach Quiche

Make this easy quiche in advance, then serve it up on busy school nights or anytime you need fast food for your family.

Serves 4

Tip

To toast pine nuts: In a small, dry skillet over medium heat, toast pine nuts, stirring constantly, for 3 to 4 minutes or until golden and fragrant. Immediately transfer to a bowl and let cool.

• **Preheat oven to 400°F (200°C)**

1	baked 9-inch (23 cm) pie crust	1
4 cups	lightly packed spinach	1 L
1 tsp	vegetable oil	5 mL
1 cup	chopped broccoli	250 mL
1	clove garlic, minced	1
2	eggs	2
1 cup	ricotta cheese	250 mL
1/4 cup	chopped onion	60 mL
2 tbsp	pine nuts, toasted (see Tip, left)	30 mL
1/2 tsp	salt	2 mL
	Freshly ground black pepper	
1/3 cup	freshly grated Parmesan cheese	75 mL

1. Rinse spinach and drain, leaving some water clinging to the leaves. Trim off tough stems. In a skillet over medium heat, sauté spinach for about 3 minutes or until just wilted. Transfer to a colander and let cool.

2. Meanwhile, return skillet to medium heat and add oil. Sauté broccoli and garlic for 3 minutes or until broccoli is bright green. Remove from heat.

3. Drain spinach well, squeezing out excess moisture. Chop spinach coarsely. In a bowl, whisk eggs until blended. Stir in spinach, broccoli mixture, ricotta, onion, pine nuts, salt, and pepper to taste.

4. Spoon into pie crust, smoothing top. Sprinkle with Parmesan cheese. Bake in preheated oven for about 20 minutes or until filling is set. Let stand for 10 minutes before cutting into wedges.

Tofu Pita Sandwiches

Tofu and zucchini are an interesting couple for a lunchtime rendezvous on the run.

Serves 2

Tip

To julienne is to cut into matchstick-shaped pieces. For this recipe, the tofu and zucchini work well when cut into about 2-inch (5 cm) long sticks, about ¼ inch (0.5 cm) square.

1 tsp	olive oil	5 mL
8 oz	firm or extra-firm tofu, julienned	250 g
½	zucchini, julienned	½
2 tsp	tamari	10 mL
½ cup	chopped seeded cucumber	125 mL
3 tbsp	sour cream	45 mL
¼ cup	diced drained sweet pickles	60 mL
1 tsp	chopped fresh dill	5 mL
	Salt and freshly ground black pepper	
2	pitas (about 6 inches/15 cm)	2

1. In a skillet, heat oil over medium heat. Sauté tofu, zucchini and tamari for about 8 minutes or until zucchini is browned and tender. Set aside.

2. In a bowl, combine cucumber, sour cream, pickles and dill. Season with salt and pepper to taste. Cut pita breads in half crosswise and open up pockets. Spoon cucumber mixture equally into pita pockets, then add tofu and zucchini.

Bagel Melt

This is for those days when every minute counts.

Serves 2 to 4

• Preheat broiler

Tip

Vacherin des Bois Francs is an artisan cheese from Quebec, Canada. This semifirm, washed-rind cheese is a good melting cheese. Other Vacherin varieties are available from France and Switzerland. Look for them at specialty cheese shops. If you have difficultly finding Vacherin, other semifirm, washed-rind cheeses or Cheddar are acceptable substitutes.

1 tbsp	vegetable oil, divided	15 mL
4	½-inch (1 cm) thick slices firm or extra-firm tofu	4
2 tsp	tamari	10 mL
2	bagels, cut in half crosswise	2
1	clove garlic, minced	1
1 cup	sliced mushrooms	250 mL
2 tbsp	finely chopped onion	30 mL
4	slices tomato	4
2 oz	Vacherin des Bois Francs cheese, other semifirm, washed-rind cheese or Cheddar cheese, cut into thin slices (see Tip, left)	60 g
	Paprika	

1. In a large skillet, heat 2 tsp (10 mL) of the oil over high heat. Add tofu slices and drizzle with tamari. Fry, turning once, for 2 to 3 minutes per side or until crisp and browned. Place 1 slice on each bagel half.

2. Add remaining oil to the skillet and reduce heat to medium. Sauté garlic, mushrooms and onion for about 5 minutes or until mushrooms are browned. Divide equally among bagel halves, spreading on top of tofu.

3. Top equally with cheese and sprinkle with paprika. Place on a baking sheet. Broil for about 3 minutes or until cheese is melted.

Cauliflower Omelet

Easy and different, this omelet recipe needs only at few simple ingredients. Add a salad on the side, and you're done.

Serves 4

Tip
You can use leftover cooked cauliflower or other vegetables. Use about 1 cup (250 mL) finely chopped vegetables.

• **Steamer basket**

1½ cups	bite-size cauliflower florets	375 mL
2 tsp	vegetable oil	10 mL
½	onion, chopped	½
1 tsp	tamari	5 mL
4	eggs	4
1 tsp	salt	5 mL
¼ tsp	curry powder	1 mL
	Freshly ground black pepper	

1. In a steamer basket set in a pot of boiling water, steam cauliflower for about 8 minutes or until tender. Chop finely.

2. In a skillet, heat oil over medium heat. Sauté onion for about 5 minutes or until softened. Stir in cauliflower and tamari.

3. In a bowl, beat eggs with salt and curry powder. Pour into skillet over cauliflower mixture and season with pepper to taste. Cook the omelet, without stirring, for about 3 minutes or until eggs are set around the edges. Cover the pan with a lid and cook for about 3 minutes or until top is set.

Three-Bean Omelet

This omelet is as pretty as it is tasty.

Serves 4

Tip
You can use 1½ cups (375 mL) of one type of bean or chickpeas instead of the mixture. Extra canned beans and chickpeas can be refrigerated in an airtight container for up to 2 days or frozen for up to 3 months.

4	eggs	4
½ cup	drained rinsed canned black beans (see Tip, left)	125 mL
½ cup	drained rinsed canned chickpeas (see Tip, left)	125 mL
½ cup	drained rinsed canned red kidney beans (see Tip, left)	125 mL
	Salt and freshly ground black pepper	
2 tsp	olive oil, divided	10 mL
1	clove garlic, chopped	1
½	red bell pepper, diced	½
¼	Spanish onion, chopped	¼

1. In a bowl, whisk eggs until blended. Stir in black beans, chickpeas and kidney beans. Season with salt and pepper to taste. Set aside.

2. In a skillet, heat half of the oil over medium heat. Sauté garlic, bell pepper and onion for about 5 minutes or until softened. Transfer to a bowl.

3. Return skillet to medium heat and add remaining oil. Pour in egg mixture and stir in onion mixture. Cook omelet, without stirring, for about 3 minutes or until eggs are set around the edges. Cover the pan with a lid and cook for about 3 minutes or until top is set.

Club Sandwich

Serve this sandwich with homemade french fries to four hungry people.

Serves 4

Tip
Cut the tofu slices lengthwise from a block of tofu to make them about the same size as your slices of bread.

1 tbsp	tamari	15 mL
1 tbsp	balsamic vinegar	15 mL
1	clove garlic, minced	1
¼ tsp	curry powder	1 mL
	Freshly ground black pepper	
4	slices tofu, each ½ inch (1 cm) thick (see Tip, left)	4
1 tbsp	oil	15 mL
12	slices whole wheat bread	12
½ cup	shredded Cheddar cheese	125 mL
¼ cup	crumbled goat cheese	60 mL
	Dijon mustard	
4	slices red onion	4
1	tomato, sliced	1
4	leaves lettuce	4

1. In a shallow dish, combine tamari, vinegar, garlic, curry powder, and pepper to taste. Add tofu, turning to coat, and marinate at room temperature for 20 minutes.

2. In a large skillet, heat oil over high heat. Fry tofu, turning once, for about 2 minutes per side or until browned.

3. Meanwhile, toast bread. Place 4 slices of toast on a work surface. Top each with a slice of tofu, then top equally with Cheddar and goat cheeses. Place another slice of toast on top. (The tofu will melt the cheeses.) Spread top layer of toast with mustard, then top with red onion, tomato and lettuce. Sandwich with remaining 4 slices of toast. Insert toothpicks into each quarter and cut diagonally into quarters.

Stuffed Tomato with Egg

Eggs and tomatoes create a blend of irresistible flavors. Serve with a loaf of crusty bread alongside.

Serves 4

Tip
French shallots are members of the onion family. They are slightly different than regular shallots with a milder flavor. If you can't find the French ones, regular shallots are a good substitute.

4	large tomatoes	4
1 tbsp	olive oil	15 mL
2	cloves garlic, finely chopped	4
2	French shallots, finely chopped (see Tip, left)	2
4	eggs	4
	Chopped fresh parsley	

1. Using a knife, remove the tops of the tomatoes, cutting toward the center. Remove enough tomato so that the egg can rest inside it. If the tomato won't stay upright, you can cut a thin layer from the bottom.

2. In a skillet, heat oil over medium heat. Sauté garlic and shallots for about 8 minutes or until they are caramelized. Spread out into a thin layer in skillet. Place tomatoes on the bed of shallots and garlic. Continue to cook for 5 minutes.

3. Break each egg into a small bowl, then drop into the hollows of the tomatoes. Cover and let cook until the eggs are done to your taste. Garnish with parsley.

Hard-Boiled Eggs with Lentils

Serve this recipe with sticky rice that you can dip into the sauce.

Serves 4

(see Tip, page 59)

¼ cup	dried Puy lentils, rinsed (see Tip, page 59)	60 mL
1 tbsp	olive oil	15 mL
1	clove garlic, chopped	1
½	onion, chopped	½
1	tomato, diced	1
1 cup	coconut milk	250 mL
¼ tsp	curry powder	1 mL
¼ tsp	paprika	1 mL
¼ tsp	ground ginger	1 mL
	Salt and freshly ground black pepper	
4	eggs, hard-boiled (see Tip, left)	4
	Paprika	

Tip

To hard-boil eggs: Place eggs in a saucepan and add enough cold water to cover by 1 inch (2.5 cm). Bring just to a boil over medium-high heat. Remove from heat, cover and let stand for 15 minutes. Run cold water into the pan until eggs are chilled. Drain and then peel off shells.

1. In a pot of boiling water, cook lentils for about 15 minutes or until tender. Drain.

2. In a skillet, heat oil over medium heat. Sauté garlic and onion for about 5 minutes or until softened. Add cooked lentils, tomato, coconut milk, curry powder, paprika, ground ginger, and salt and black pepper to taste. Bring to a boil, stirring. Reduce heat and boil gently, stirring often, for about 5 minutes or until flavors are blended.

3. Pour mixture into a serving dish. Cut eggs in two and lay on top of the mixture. Garnish with additional paprika.

Frittata

An excellent recipe for using leftover pasta, this nourishing dish has a slightly different texture than most omelets, thanks to the pasta.

Serves 4

Tip

When you're making a spaghetti meal, cook extra pasta for this frittata. Rinse the spaghetti under cool running water and drain well. Toss with a small amount of olive oil, then refrigerate in an airtight container for up to 3 days.

1 tbsp	olive oil	15 mL
3 cups	cooked whole wheat spaghetti	750 mL
1	clove garlic, minced	1
1 tsp	tamari	5 mL
1	onion, sliced	1
½	red bell pepper, diced	½
4	eggs	4
1 tsp	salt	5 mL
	Freshly ground black pepper	

1. In a skillet, heat oil over medium heat. Add spaghetti, garlic and tamari and cook, stirring gently, for 2 to 3 minutes or until heated through. Transfer to a bowl and set aside.

2. In same skillet, sauté onion and bell pepper for 2 to 3 minutes or until softened. Return pasta mixture to skillet and spread evenly.

3. In a small bowl, beat eggs until blended. Pour evenly over pasta mixture and cook, stirring gently, for about 3 minutes or until eggs start to set. Cook, without stirring, for about 7 minutes longer or until eggs are just set. Season with salt, and pepper to taste. Let stand for 3 minutes before serving.

All-Dressed Pizza

Pizza is child's play when you do it the pita way.

Serves 4

Tip

If you have picky eaters in your family, let them choose which vegetables and cheese they'd like and have them assemble their own custom pizza — they'll be much more enthusiastic to eat their own creation.

- **Preheat oven to 400°F (200°C)**

1 tbsp	olive oil	15 mL
8 oz	firm or extra-firm tofu, crumbled	250 g
2	carrots, diced	2
1	onion, chopped	1
1	zucchini, diced	1
1	red bell pepper, cut into strips	1
1 cup	tomato sauce	250 mL
4	pitas, each about 6 inches (15 cm)	4
1 cup	shredded sharp (aged) Cheddar cheese	250 mL
1 cup	shredded Havarti cheese	250 mL
	Paprika	

1. In a skillet, heat oil over high heat. Sauté tofu for about 3 minutes or until starting to brown. Add carrots, onion, zucchini and bell pepper and sauté for about 3 minutes or until softened. Remove from heat.

2. Spread tomato sauce evenly on the pitas and place on a baking sheet. Divide vegetable mixture equally over top and sprinkle with Cheddar and Havarti. Sprinkle with paprika.

3. Bake in preheated oven for about 15 minutes or until pitas are toasted. Broil for about 2 minutes or until cheese is browned.

Four-Cheese Pizza

Choose this version for cheese lovers, and use a high-quality tomato sauce.

Serves 4

Tip

If you have homemade tomato sauce, just make sure it's thick enough to stay on the pizza. If it's a bit thin, stir in a small amount of tomato paste. When purchasing tomato sauce, check the nutrition information on the label and choose the one lowest in sodium and sugar.

• **Preheat oven to 400°F (200°C)**

1 cup	tomato sauce (see Tip, left)	250 mL
4	pitas, each about 6 inches (15 cm)	4
¾ cup	shredded sharp (old) Cheddar cheese	175 mL
¾ cup	shredded Havarti cheese	175 mL
½ cup	crumbled creamy goat cheese	125 mL
¼ cup	freshly grated Parmesan cheese	60 mL
	Paprika	

1. Spread tomato sauce on pita bread and place on a baking sheet. Divide Cheddar and Havarti cheese equally on top, then goat cheese and Parmesan cheese. Sprinkle with paprika.

2. Bake in preheated oven for about 15 minutes or until pitas are toasted. Broil for about 2 minutes or until cheese is browned.

Variation

Zesty Four-Cheese Pizza: Use a spicy tomato sauce and replace the Cheddar and Havarti cheeses with ¼ cup (60 mL) each crumbled blue cheese and freshly shredded Asiago cheese.

Pesto Pizza

It's the best pizza in town. And it's easy!

Serves 4

• **Preheat oven to 400°F (200°C)**

¼ cup	Basil Pesto (page 73) or store-bought (see Tip, left)	60 mL
4	large flour tortillas	4
2	tomatoes, sliced very thin	2
2 cups	shredded sharp (aged) Cheddar cheese	500 mL

1. Spread pesto equally over one side of tortillas and place on a baking sheet. Arrange tomato slices on top and sprinkle with cheese.

2. Bake in preheated oven for about 15 minutes or until tortillas are toasted and cheese is melted.

Variation

Double-Tomato Pesto Pizza: Use sun-dried tomato pesto instead of basil pesto and replace the Cheddar with shredded mozzarella cheese.

Tips

Pesto is a magical mixture — of basil leaves, garlic, olive oil and pine nuts — which originated in Italy. The word "pesto" means "ground." Traditionally, the ingredients were ground in a mortar.

You will not use all the pesto in this recipe. You can freeze the remainder in small plastic containers, each about ½ cup (125 mL), until you need it. I make a large quantity of pesto in the summer, using fresh basil, to supply me for the year.

Burritos

Roll up this sauce in tortillas and generously dollop with sour cream. Decadent!

Serves 4

Tip

Canned beans are a terrific base for many meals. Always drain and rinse canned beans before using. If you don't use the whole can, store them in an airtight container for up to 2 days or freeze for up to 3 months.

1 tbsp	olive oil	15 mL
1	clove garlic, chopped	1
1	onion, chopped	1
1	red bell pepper, diced	1
½	zucchini, diced	½
1	can (14 oz/398 mL) plum (Roma) tomatoes	1
1	can (10 oz/284 mL) mushrooms, drained	1
1 cup	drained rinsed canned black beans (see Tip, left)	250 mL
1 tsp	herbes de Provence (see Tip, page 47)	5 mL
	Freshly ground black pepper	
8	large flour tortillas	8

1. In a large skillet, heat oil over medium heat. Sauté garlic and onion for about 5 minutes or until softened.

2. Add bell pepper and zucchini and sauté for 3 minutes or until tender-crisp. Stir in tomatoes, mushrooms, beans, herbes de Provence, and black pepper to taste, and bring to a boil. Reduce heat and simmer, stirring and breaking up tomatoes with a spoon, for about 15 minutes or until thick.

3. Spoon sauce equally along the centre of tortillas and roll up.

Chickpea Stew

Yogurt makes all the difference in this stew. Serve this dish with simple white rice.

Serves 4

> **Tip**
> Use full-fat plain yogurt for the best texture in this stew. Lower fat yogurt may split and make the stew watery and curdled.

1 tbsp	olive oil	15 mL
2	cloves garlic, chopped	2
1	onion, chopped	1
½ cup	diced turnip	125 mL
½ cup	diced carrot	125 mL
1	can (14 to 19 oz/398 to 540 mL) chickpeas, drained and rinsed	1
1	can (14 oz/398 mL) plum (Roma) tomatoes	1
20	leaves spinach	20
½ cup	full-fat plain yogurt (see Tip, left)	125 mL
1 tsp	ground coriander	5 mL
½ tsp	ground turmeric	2 mL
½ tsp	paprika	2 mL
⅛ tsp	ground cumin	0.5 mL
	Salt and freshly ground black pepper	

1. In a large pot, heat oil over medium heat. Sauté garlic and onion for about 7 minutes or until starting to turn golden. Add turnip and carrot and sauté for 5 minutes or until starting to soften.

2. Stir in chickpeas, tomatoes, spinach, yogurt, coriander, turmeric, paprika, cumin, and salt and black pepper to taste. Bring to a simmer, stirring often. Reduce heat and simmer, stirring occasionally, for about 20 minutes or until flavors are blended.

Mini Lasagnas

Here's how to make individual lasagnas, which won't sink under the weight of their calories.

Serves 4

Tip

Cans of Italian tomatoes are a great pantry item to have on hand. They are far less expensive and more flavorful than tomatoes out of season and require no preparation. If you open a can and don't need all of the tomatoes at once, transfer the extras to an airtight container and refrigerate for up to 3 days or freeze for up to 6 months.

- Preheat oven to 400°F (200°C)
- Four 2-cup (500 mL) baking dishes, greased

10	lasagna noodles, preferably with curly edges	10
1 tbsp	olive oil, divided	15 mL
½	onion, chopped	½
1 cup	canned plum (Roma) tomatoes (see Tip, left)	250 mL
4	slices tofu, each ½ inch (1 cm) thick	4
	Tamari to taste	
8	mushrooms, sliced	8
4	slices Brie cheese	4
4	slices tomato	4

1. In a large pot of boiling salted water, cook lasagna noodles according to package directions until tender but firm. Drain and cut crosswise in half. Set aside.

2. In a small saucepan, heat 1 tsp (5 mL) of the oil over medium heat. Sauté onion for about 5 minutes or until softened. Add tomatoes and bring to a boil, breaking up with a spoon. Reduce heat and simmer for 5 to 10 minutes or until slightly thickened. Set aside.

3. In a skillet, heat 1 tsp (5 mL) of oil over medium-high heat. Fry tofu slices, turning once, for about 3 minutes per side or until browned. Season with tamari to taste. Transfer to a plate. Add remaining oil to skillet and sauté mushrooms for about 8 minutes or until liquid is released and mushrooms are browned. Remove from heat.

Tips

Tips

For extra fiber and nutrients, use whole wheat lasagna noodles.

For a more pronounced mushroom flavor, use 8 cremini mushrooms or 2 cups (500 mL) chopped portobello mushroom caps.

4. In each prepared dish, layer the following ingredients: lasagna, half the mushrooms and some sauce, more lasagna, tofu, lasagna, the rest of the mushrooms and sauce, lasagna, and finally Brie cheese and a dash of sauce as garnish. Top with tomato slices.

5. Bake in preheated oven until cheese is melted.

Variation

Zucchini Roasted Red Pepper Mini Lasagnas: Replace the mushrooms with 1 diced zucchini, add 1 roasted red bell pepper, chopped, with the zucchini when assembling lasagnas and use 1 cup (250 mL) shredded smoked or regular mozzarella cheese in place of the Brie.

Creamy Lentils

Lentils are a great addition to many sauces, and are a special treat in a creamy sauce.

Serves 4

Tip

Garam masala is an Indian spice mixture that can include up to 12 spices, including a traditional mix of coriander seeds, cumin seeds, peppercorns, cinnamon, cardamom pods and cloves.

1½ cups	dried Puy lentils, rinsed (see Tip, page 109)	375 mL
1 tbsp	olive oil	15 mL
2	cloves garlic, chopped	2
½	onion, chopped	½
½	zucchini, diced	½
1	can (14 oz/398 mL) plum (Roma) tomatoes	1
½ tsp	garam masala (see Tip, left)	2 mL
½ tsp	curry powder	2 mL
¼ tsp	herbes de Provence	1 mL
3 tbsp	creamy goat cheese	45 mL

1. In a pot of boiling water, cook lentils for about 15 minutes or until tender. Drain.

2. In a skillet, heat oil over medium heat. Sauté garlic, onion and zucchini for about 7 minutes or until starting to brown. Stir in lentils, tomatoes, garam masala, curry powder and herbes de Provence and bring to a boil. Reduce heat and simmer, stirring often and breaking up tomatoes with a spoon, for about 10 minutes or until thickened and flavors are blended. Stir in cheese until melted and sauce is creamy.

Lentils with Cumin

If you do not have the time, omit the rice and double the amount of the lentils.

Serves 4

Tip

Puy lentils are tiny, French green lentils and are often found at specialty stores. If you can't find them, use regular dried green or brown lentils and increase the cooking time by 5 to 10 minutes.

½ cup	dried Puy lentils (see Tip, left)	125 mL
½ cup	wild rice, cooked	125 mL
1 tbsp	olive oil	15 mL
1	onion, chopped	1
1	clove garlic, minced	1
1	carrot, diced	1
1	zucchini, diced	1
½	green bell pepper, diced	½
1	can (14 oz/398 mL) plum (Roma) tomatoes	1
1 tsp	ground cumin	5 mL
½ tsp	paprika	2 mL
½ tsp	salt	2 mL
¼ tsp	ground ginger	1 mL
½ cup	light sour cream	125 mL

1. In a large pot of boiling water, cook lentils for about 15 minutes or until tender. Drain well.

2. In a medium pot, heat oil over medium heat. Sauté onion, garlic, carrot, zucchini and bell pepper for about 8 minutes or until softened.

3. Stir in tomatoes, cumin, paprika, salt and ginger and bring to a boil, breaking up tomatoes with a spoon. Stir in lentils and wild rice. You can add ¼ cup (60 mL) water if the mixture is too thick. Reduce heat and simmer, stirring occasionally, for 15 minutes or until flavors are blended. Stir in sour cream just before serving.

Lentil Ratatouille

At the end of summer, when eggplant and zucchini are in season, make a bigger batch of this special ratatouille, and celebrate the harvest with your neighbors.

Serves 8

Tip
Cut your vegetables in large pieces so that they are pleasing to bite into.

3 tbsp	olive oil, divided	45 mL
2	cloves garlic, chopped	2
1	onion, chopped	1
4 cups	chopped small eggplants	1 L
4 cups	chopped zucchini	1 L
4 cups	chopped carrots	1 L
¾ cup	dried Puy lentils (see Tip, page 109)	175 mL
1	can (28 oz/796 mL) plum (Roma) tomatoes	1
4	tomatoes	4
½ cup	water	125 mL
1 tsp	dried parsley	5 mL
1 tsp	dried basil	5 mL
½ tsp	dried oregano	2 mL
2	bay leaves	2
2 tsp	salt	10 mL

1. In a pot, heat 1 tbsp (15 mL) of the oil over medium heat. Sauté garlic and onion for about 5 minutes or until softened. Add remaining oil to pot. Stir in eggplant, zucchini, carrot, lentils, plum tomatoes, tomatoes, water, parsley, basil, oregano, bay leaves and salt and bring to a boil, stirring.

2. Reduce heat and simmer, stirring often for 10 to 20 minutes, until vegetables are cooked to your taste. You can add a little water if you want a more juicy ratatouille. Discard bay leaves.

Chili sin Carne

Here is my vegetarian version of this spicy, sunny recipe. You can present this chili in a loaf of bread.

Serves 6

Tip

If you don't have crushed or ground tomatoes, you can purée a can of whole tomatoes in a blender, food processor or using an immersion blender.

1 tbsp	olive oil	15 mL
1	clove garlic, chopped	1
1	onion, chopped	1
1	carrot, diced	1
1	zucchini, diced	1
1	can (28 oz/796 mL) crushed (ground) tomatoes	1
1	can (14 to 19 oz/398 to 540 mL) red kidney beans, drained and rinsed	1
2 cups	frozen corn kernels	500 mL
1½ cups	water	375 mL
1 tbsp	granulated sugar	15 mL
1	dried chile pepper, crumbled	1
1 tsp	ground coriander	5 mL
1 tsp	dried parsley	5 mL
1 tsp	dried basil	5 mL
½ tsp	paprika	2 mL

1. In a large pot, heat oil over medium heat. Sauté garlic and onion for about 5 minutes or until softened. Add carrot and zucchini and sauté for about 5 minutes or until softened. Stir in tomatoes, beans, corn, water, sugar, chile pepper, coriander, parsley, basil and paprika and bring to a boil, stirring often.

2. Reduce heat and simmer, stirring often, for about 20 minutes or until flavors are blended.

Spaghetti Sauce

This sauce is very simple way to introduce your children to tofu — they won't even notice it.

Serves 6 to 8

Tips

The block-style tofu comes in different textures: medium, firm and extra-firm. You can often interchange firm and extra-firm in recipes according to your own preference.

When purchasing canned tomatoes and tomato sauce, check the nutrition information and choose those that are lowest in sodium.

1 tbsp	olive oil	15 mL
½	Spanish onion, chopped	½
½	zucchini, diced	½
5	cloves garlic, chopped	5
5 oz	firm or extra-firm tofu, crumbled (see Tips, left)	150 g
1 tbsp	soy sauce	15 mL
1	can (5½ oz/156 mL) tomato paste	1
1	can (28 oz/796 mL) plum (Roma) tomatoes	1
1	can (14 oz/398 mL) tomato sauce	1
3	carrots, diced	3
1	stalk celery, diced	1
1 tbsp	granulated sugar	15 mL
5	whole cloves	5
Pinch	cayenne pepper	Pinch
Pinch	ground cinnamon	Pinch
3	bay leaves	3
	Salt and freshly ground black pepper	

1. In a pot, heat oil over medium heat. Sauté onion for about 8 minutes or until lightly caramelized.

2. Add zucchini and garlic and sauté for 5 minutes or until softened. Stir in tofu and soy sauce and sauté for 2 minutes.

3. Stir in tomato paste until blended. Stir in plum tomatoes, tomato sauce, carrots, celery, sugar, cloves, cayenne pepper, cinnamon, bay leaves, and salt and black pepper to taste, and bring to a boil, breaking up tomatoes with a spoon.

4. Reduce heat and simmer, stirring often, for about 20 minutes or until thickened and carrots are tender. Discard cloves and bay leaves.

Tofu Tacos

The kind of recipe we love, these tacos have plenty of crunch.

Serves 4 to 6

Tip

To toast sesame seeds:
Place seeds on a
baking sheet and toast
in a preheated 350°F
(180°C) oven, stirring
once or twice, for
about 5 minutes or until
fragrant and golden.

1 tbsp	olive oil	15 mL
1	onion, chopped	1
1	clove garlic, chopped	1
8 oz	firm tofu, drained (about ½ block)	250 g
1 cup	diced tomato	250 mL
6	mushrooms, sliced	6
1	carrot, grated	1
½	zucchini, grated	½
1 tbsp	tamari	15 mL
1 tbsp	sesame seeds, toasted (see Tip, left)	15 mL
12	taco shells	12

1. In a large skillet, heat oil over medium heat. Sauté onion and garlic for about 7 minutes or until golden.

2. Add tofu, tomato, mushrooms, carrot, zucchini and tamari and sauté for about 6 minutes or until vegetables are softened.

3. Sprinkle toasted sesame seeds on top. Fill taco shells equally with mixture.

Green Pasta

Baby green peas and lemon juice liven up this pasta with freshness and flavor.

Serves 4

Tip

If you don't have time to make broth from scratch, the ready-to-use broth in Tetra Paks is a convenient alternative. The flavor varies by brand so do some experimenting and try out different brands to find one you like. Check the nutritional panel to choose one that is lowest in sodium.

1 lb	fusilli pasta	500 g
1 tbsp	olive oil	15 mL
5	green onions, sliced	5
8 oz	firm or extra-firm tofu, cubed (see Tips, page 112)	250 g
1 tbsp	tamari	15 mL
1	zucchini, diced	1
2 cups	green beans, cut in half	500 mL
½ cup	frozen green peas	125 mL
1 tsp	cornstarch	5 mL
¾ cup	vegetable broth (see Tip, left)	175 mL
1 tsp	grated fresh gingerroot	5 mL
2 tbsp	freshly squeezed lemon juice	30 mL
	Salt and freshly ground black pepper	

1. In a large pot of boiling salted water, cook pasta for about 10 minutes or until tender but firm. Drain well and rinse. Drain again.

2. Meanwhile, in a large skillet, heat oil over medium heat. Sauté green onions, tofu and tamari for about 5 minutes or until tofu starts to brown. Stir in green beans and peas.

3. Whisk cornstarch into broth and pour into skillet. Stir in ginger, lemon juice and salt and black pepper to taste. Simmer, stirring often, for about 5 minutes or until vegetables are tender. Serve over pasta.

Blue Pasta

Blue cheese takes center stage in this mouthwatering recipe.

Serves 4

Tip

To toast pine nuts:
In a small, dry skillet over medium heat, toast pine nuts, stirring constantly, for 3 to 4 minutes or until golden and fragrant. Immediately transfer to a bowl and let cool.

1 lb	linguini pasta	500 g
1 tbsp	olive oil	15 mL
5	green onions, sliced	5
1	clove garlic, minced	1
1½ cups	milk	375 mL
¾ cup	crumbled blue cheese	175 mL
4 oz	spinach, trimmed	125 g
2 tbsp	pine nuts, toasted (see Tip, left)	30 mL

1. In a large pot of boiling salted water, cook pasta for about 10 minutes or until tender but firm. Drain and rinse under hot water. Drain again.

2. Meanwhile, in a skillet, heat oil over medium heat. Sauté green onions and garlic for about 5 minutes or until golden. Stir in milk, blue cheese and spinach and simmer for about 10 minutes or until slightly reduced (do not let boil).

3. Serve sauce over pasta and sprinkle with pine nuts.

Red Pasta

A quick-fix recipe, this only takes about 20 minutes to prepare.

Serves 4

Tip
Whole wheat pasta is a terrific way to include extra nutrients and fiber in your meals. If your family isn't used to eating it, introduce it by mixing a small amount with regular white pasta then gradually increase the proportion of whole wheat as you become accustomed to the flavor and texture.

• **Food processor**

1 lb	rigatoni pasta (see Tip, left)	500 g
2 tbsp	olive oil	30 mL
2	cloves garlic, chopped	2
1	onion, chopped	1
1	can (28 oz/796 mL) plum (Roma) tomatoes	1
¼ cup	cream cheese	60 mL
	Salt and freshly ground black pepper	

1. In a large pot of boiling salted water, cook pasta for about 10 minutes or until tender but firm. Drain and rinse under hot water. Drain again.

2. In a saucepan, heat oil over medium heat. Sauté garlic and onion for about 8 minutes or until golden. Stir in tomatoes and bring to a boil. Reduce heat and simmer for about 15 minutes or until thickened.

3. Transfer sauce to a food processor and purée until smooth. Add cream cheese and process until melted and creamy. Season with salt and pepper to taste. Serve immediately over pasta.

Pasta with Goat Cheese

Discover the delightful texture of Japanese soba noodles in a scrumptious sauce.

Serves 2

Tip
If you do not have soba noodles, you can substitute spaghettini.

- **Preheat oven to 400°F (200°C)**
- **Large baking dish**

8 oz	soba noodles (see Tip, left)	250 g
3 tbsp	Basil Pesto (see page 73) or store-bought	45 mL
1 tsp	olive oil	5 mL
4	green onions, chopped	4
2	cloves garlic, chopped	2
1	zucchini, thinly sliced	1
2	tomatoes, diced	2
1/3 cup	crumbled creamy goat cheese	75 mL

1. In a large pot of boiling salted water, cook noodles for about 6 minutes or until tender but firm. Drain and rinse under hot water. Drain again and transfer to a large baking dish. Add pesto and toss to coat.

2. In a skillet, heat oil over medium heat. Sauté green onions and garlic for about 3 minutes or until softened. Stir in zucchini, tomatoes and goat cheese and cook, stirring, for about 3 minutes or until zucchini is warmed and cheese is melted.

3. Add vegetables to noodles and toss to coat. Bake in preheated oven for about 10 minutes or until noodles are slightly crispy.

Macaroni with Tomato and Cheese

It's important to use a sharp Cheddar to enjoy the full flavor of this recipe.

Serves 4

Tip

Caramelizing the onions and garlic until they're very dark gives a rich flavor to the sauce. Do keep the ingredients in the pan in motion by stirring constantly so they brown evenly.

1 lb	whole wheat elbow macaroni	500 g
1 tbsp	olive oil	15 mL
1	onion, finely chopped	1
4	cloves garlic, finely chopped	4
1	can (28 oz/796 mL) diced plum (Roma) tomatoes	1
¼ cup	water	60 mL
1 cup	shredded sharp (aged) Cheddar cheese	250 mL
Pinch	cayenne pepper	Pinch

1. In a large pot of boiling salted water, cook pasta for about 10 minutes or until tender but firm. Drain and rinse under hot water. Drain again.

2. Meanwhile, in a skillet, heat oil over medium heat. Sauté onion for about 7 minutes or until browned. Add garlic and sauté until caramelized (almost black). Stir in tomatoes and water and bring to a boil. Reduce heat and simmer, without stirring, for 20 minutes (you can shake the skillet from time to time).

3. Stir in cheese and cayenne pepper just until cheese is still visible to the eye. Serve over pasta.

Pecan Paradise Pasta

The aroma and melt-in-your-mouth flavors of this dish are worthy of a place in paradise.

Serves 4

Tip

Cheddar cheese made from goat's milk has a distinctive, pungent flavor and firm texture rather than the more typical soft, creamy texture of goat's cheese. Look for it at specialty cheese shops or in the deli sections of well-stocked supermarkets.

• **Food processor**

1 lb	whole wheat spaghetti	500 g
1 cup	pecan halves	250 mL
1	slice whole wheat bread, crust removed	1
½ cup	fresh parsley leaves	125 mL
2	cloves garlic	2
⅓ cup	olive oil	75 mL
3 tbsp	melted butter	45 mL
	Finely shredded goat Cheddar cheese (see Tip, left)	

1. In a large pot of boiling salted water, cook pasta for about 10 minutes. Drain and rinse under hot water. Drain again.

2. Meanwhile, in a dry skillet over medium heat, toast pecans, stirring constantly for about 5 minutes or until golden and fragrant. Immediately transfer to a bowl and let cool.

3. Toast bread in toaster.

4. In a food processor, process pecans, toast, parsley, garlic, oil and melted butter just long enough so that the texture remains fairly crunchy. Serve over pasta. Top with goat Cheddar cheese.

Couscous with Prunes

Prunes add their sweetness to this divine couscous. Cut the vegetables according to your own preference in shapes and sizes.

Serves 4

Tip

Canned chickpeas are a terrific base for many meals. Always drain and rinse canned beans before using. If you don't use the whole can, store them in an airtight container for up to 2 days or freeze for up to 3 months.

1 tbsp	olive oil, divided	15 mL
2	cloves garlic, chopped	2
1	onion, chopped	1
1	red bell pepper, coarsely chopped	1
3	carrots, diced	3
2 cups	diced winter squash	500 mL
1/2 cup	diced turnip	125 mL
1 cup	cubed sweet potato	250 mL
1/2 cup	prunes, cut in half	125 mL
1/2 cup	drained rinsed canned chickpeas (see Tip, left)	125 mL
1 cup	canned plum (Roma) tomatoes (see Tip, right)	250 mL
1 cup	vegetable broth	250 mL
1	zucchini, diced	1
1/2 tsp	ground coriander	2 mL
1/2 tsp	turmeric	2 mL
1/2 tsp	paprika	2 mL
1/2 tsp	salt	2 mL
	Freshly ground black pepper	
2 cups	water	500 mL
2 cups	couscous	500 mL

1. In a saucepan, heat 2 tsp (10 mL) of the oil over medium heat. Sauté garlic and onion for about 5 minutes or until softened. Add bell pepper, carrots, squash, turnip and sweet potato and sauté for about 5 minutes or until starting to soften. Stir in prunes, chickpeas, tomatoes, zucchini, coriander, turmeric, paprika and salt. Reduce heat to medium-low, cover and simmer, stirring often, for about 15 minutes or until vegetables are tender.

2. Meanwhile, in a saucepan, bring water to a boil over high heat. Gradually pour in couscous and remaining olive oil. Remove from heat, cover and let stand for 5 minutes or until couscous is softened and liquid has been absorbed. Fluff with a fork. Spoon vegetable mixture over couscous.

Variation

Ratatouille with Bulgur: Omit the winter squash, prunes, coriander and turmeric. Add 2 cups (500 mL) diced peeled eggplant with the onion and 2 tsp (10 mL) dried herbes de Provence with the paprika. Substitute fine or coarse bulgur for the couscous and cook according to package directions.

Spinach Ricotta Cannelloni

Don't have much time? This recipe takes just a few steps.

Makes 8 small cannelloni

Tip
The flat lasagna noodles without curly edges work best for this recipe.

- **Preheat broiler**
- **8-inch (20 cm) square glass baking dish, greased**

4	spinach lasagna noodles (see Tip, left)	4
Filling		
1 tsp	olive oil	5 mL
1	onion, chopped	1
1	clove garlic, chopped	1
3 cups	fresh spinach, chopped	750 mL
1/2 cup	ricotta cheese	125 mL
Béchamel		
2 tbsp	butter	30 mL
2 tbsp	all-purpose flour	30 mL
1 1/4 cups	milk	300 mL
	Salt and freshly ground black pepper	
1 cup	shredded Emmental cheese	250 mL
	Paprika	

1. In a large pot of boiling salted water, cook lasagna noodles according to package directions until tender but firm. Drain and rinse under hot water. Drain well and cut crosswise in half.

2. *Filling:* In a skillet, heat oil over medium heat. Sauté garlic and onion for about 5 minutes or until softened. Stir in spinach until wilted. Remove from heat and stir in ricotta.

3. Spoon filling equally onto one end of each piece of lasagna, roll up and place in a baking dish, seam side down.

4. *Béchamel:* In a saucepan, melt butter over medium heat. Sprinkle with flour and sauté for 30 seconds. Gradually whisk in milk and bring to a simmer, whisking constantly. Simmer, stirring, for about 5 minutes or until thickened. Season with salt and black pepper to taste.

5. Pour béchamel evenly over cannelloni. Top with cheese and a little paprika. Broil for about 5 minutes or until cheese is melted and browned.

Variation

Spinach, Roasted Pepper and Basil Cannelloni:
Reduce the spinach to 2 cups (500 mL) and add 1 roasted red bell pepper, finely chopped, with the ricotta. Stir $1/4$ cup (60 mL) finely chopped fresh basil into the béchamel with the salt and pepper.

Curry Couscous

We often forget the couscous in the cupboard, but it's a fast, easy and affordable base for many delicious dishes.

Serves 2 to 4

Tip

To toast almonds: In a small, dry skillet over medium heat, toast almonds, stirring constantly, for 3 to 4 minutes or until golden and fragrant. Immediately transfer to a bowl and let cool.

1 cup	water	250 mL
1 cup	couscous	250 mL
3 tbsp	olive oil, divided	45 mL
1	onion, chopped	1
1	clove garlic, chopped	1
1 cup	frozen green peas	250 mL
1 cup	frozen corn kernels	250 mL
½ cup	golden raisins	125 mL
1 tbsp	curry powder	15 mL
1 tsp	brown sugar	5 mL
½ tsp	salt	2 mL
½ tsp	ground coriander	2 mL
2 tbsp	white vinegar	30 mL
1 tbsp	tamari	15 mL
½ cup	slivered almonds, toasted (see Tip, left)	125 mL

1. In a saucepan, bring water to a boil over high heat. Gradually stir in couscous and 1 tsp (5 mL) of the oil. Remove from heat, cover and let stand for 5 minutes or until couscous is softened and liquid has been absorbed. Fluff with a fork.

2. Meanwhile, in a large skillet, heat remaining oil over medium heat. Sauté onion and garlic for about 5 minutes or until softened. Stir in peas, corn, raisins, curry powder, brown sugar, salt, coriander, vinegar and tamari and sauté for about 5 minutes or until peas and corn are hot.

3. Add couscous and increase heat to high. Cook, stirring gently, for about 5 minutes or until flavors are blended. Sprinkle with toasted almonds. Serve hot or cold.

Tofu with Peanut Sauce

For this little delicacy it's important to cook the cubes of tofu over fairly high heat so they become crispy on the outside, but stay soft on the inside. This recipe is good hot or cold, accompanied by rice or salad.

Serves 4

Tip

The peanut sauce can also be served cold. Transfer to a bowl, cover and refrigerate for at least 1 hour or for up to 2 days.

Peanut Sauce

¾ cup	coconut milk	175 mL
¼ cup	peanut butter	60 mL
2 tbsp	vegetable broth	30 mL
2 tbsp	soy sauce	30 mL
2 tbsp	tahini	30 mL
1	clove garlic, minced	1
1 tsp	sesame oil	5 mL
1 tsp	rice vinegar	5 mL
2 tsp	granulated sugar	10 mL
1 tsp	ground ginger	5 mL
	Cayenne pepper	

Tofu

1 tbsp	olive oil	15 mL
1 lb	firm tofu, cubed	500 g
2 tsp	tamari	10 mL

1. *Peanut Sauce:* In a saucepan, whisk together coconut milk, peanut butter, vegetable broth, soy sauce, tahini, garlic, sesame oil, rice vinegar, sugar, ground ginger and cayenne pepper. Heat over medium heat, whisking constantly, until bubbling.

2. *Tofu:* In a skillet, heat oil over high heat. Sauté tofu for about 5 minutes or until golden and crisp. Stir in tamari. Serve hot tofu with peanut sauce.

Tofu Brochettes

This summertime recipe that gets you outdoors and cooking on the barbecue. Serve on a bed of rice or with a salad.

Makes 6 brochettes

Tip

Tamari is a sauce made from soybeans. It is thicker and richer in flavor than soy sauce. To keep the sodium level in check, look for sodium-reduced versions. If you don't have tamari, sodium-reduced soy sauce can be substituted with a pinch of sugar or drop of honey.

- **Preheat greased barbecue grill to medium**
- **Six 10- to 12-inch (25 to 30 cm) skewers, soaked if bamboo**

1 lb	extra-firm tofu	500 g
1	red bell pepper	1
1	green bell pepper	1
2	zucchini	2
½	red onion	½
12	cherry tomatoes	12
12	button mushrooms, stems removed	12
¼ cup	tamari (see Tip, left)	60 mL
¼ cup	olive oil	60 mL
2 tbsp	balsamic vinegar	30 mL
3	cloves garlic, minced	3
1 tbsp	curry powder	15 mL

1. Cut tofu into cubes and cut red pepper, green pepper, zucchini and red onion into large pieces. Leave cherry tomatoes and mushrooms whole.

2. In a bowl, combine tamari, oil, vinegar, garlic and curry powder. Add tofu and vegetables and toss to coat. Let stand for at least 10 minutes or cover and refrigerate for up to 1 day, stirring from time to time.

3. Remove tofu and vegetables from marinade, reserving marinade. Thread alternately on skewers (position red onion next to the tofu for optimal flavor).

4. Place on preheated grill and grill, turning often and basting with reserved marinade for about 10 minutes or until vegetables are tender.

Vegetable Stir-Fry

Here is a recipe inspired by Asian vegetable stir-fries. The roasted peanuts add color, crunch and flavor.

Serves 2 to 3

Tip

Stir-fries are easy to customize to your taste. For a milder flavor, decrease or omit the chile pepper, or change-up the vegetables using your favorites and what's in season — just keep the quantity similar so there's enough sauce to coat and flavor them.

1 tbsp	olive oil	15 mL
1	onion, chopped	1
1	clove garlic, chopped	1
8 oz	medium tofu, drained	250 g
2	carrots, diced	2
1	can (4 oz/113 mL) water chestnuts, drained and sliced	1
1	fresh hot chile pepper, seeded and coarsely chopped	1
4 oz	sliced mushrooms	125 g
3 tbsp	tamari	45 mL
1 tbsp	rice vinegar	15 mL
1 tbsp	brown sugar	15 mL
1 tbsp	tahini paste	15 mL
1 tsp	ground ginger	5 mL
2 cups	finely chopped broccoli	500 mL
1 cup	bean sprouts	250 mL
1/4 cup	roasted peanuts	60 mL
	Chopped cilantro, optional	

1. In a wok or a large skillet, heat oil over medium–high heat. Sauté onion and garlic for about 5 minutes or until golden. Add tofu, carrots, water chestnuts, chile pepper, mushrooms, tamari, vinegar, brown sugar, tahini and ginger and stir-fry, breaking up tofu into bite-size pieces, for 5 to 6 minutes or until vegetables are softened.

2. Add broccoli, bean sprouts and peanuts and stir-fry for about 3 minutes or until broccoli is tender-crisp. Garnish with a few cilantro leaves, if desired.

Vegetable Curry

The broth in this vegetable curry is delicious and — good news — it's not greasy.

Serves 4

Tip
This curry tastes even better the next day! Transfer to a shallow container and let cool. Cover and refrigerate for up to 2 days, then reheat in a saucepan over medium heat, stirring often, until hot and bubbling.

1 tbsp	olive oil	15 mL
1	onion, chopped	1
2	cloves garlic, chopped	1
1 cup	diced sweet potato	250 mL
3	carrots, sliced	3
1	can (4 oz/113 mL) water chestnuts, drained and sliced	1
1	fresh hot chile pepper, seeded and minced	1
1/2	green bell pepper, diced	1/2
1 cup	coconut milk	250 mL
1 cup	vegetable broth	250 mL
2 tsp	ground coriander	10 mL
1 tsp	ground ginger	5 mL
1 tsp	ground cumin	5 mL
1 tsp	salt	5 mL
	Freshly ground black pepper	
1 cup	diced zucchini	250 mL
3 cups	chopped broccoli	750 mL
5	large white mushrooms	5

1. In a large pot, heat oil over medium heat. Sauté onion for about 5 minutes or until softened. Add garlic, sweet potato, carrots, water chestnuts, chile pepper and bell pepper and sauté for about 5 minutes or until carrots start to soften.

2. Stir in coconut milk and vegetable broth. Stir in coriander, ginger, cumin, salt, and black pepper to taste. Bring to a boil, stirring often. Stir in zucchini, broccoli and mushrooms. Reduce heat and simmer for about 10 minutes or until vegetables are tender.

Spinach Ricotta Cannelloni (page 122)

Tofu with Peanut Sauce (page 125)

Tofu Brochettes (page 126)

Cheese Fondue (page 130)

Polenta Mountain (page 132)

Vegetable Paella (page 135)

Stuffed Squash (page 136)

Stuffed Peppers (page 137)

Veggie Burger

Here is a recipe with a tofu and potato base that doesn't try to imitate the taste of the classic hamburger!

Serves 4

Tip

Tahini is a paste made from sesame seeds. It is used in traditional hummus and to add a special touch to Asian dressings.

• **Food processor**

8 oz	firm tofu, cut into chunks	250 g
2	potatoes, grated	2
2	cloves garlic	2
1	small onion, cut into chunks	1
1/4 cup	large-flake (old-fashioned) rolled oats	60 mL
1/4 cup	all-purpose flour	60 mL
1/4 cup	soy sauce	60 mL
2 tbsp	tahini (see Tip, left)	30 mL
1 tsp	Dijon mustard	5 mL
1/4 cup	sunflower seeds	60 mL
2 tbsp	olive oil	30 mL
4	hamburger buns, split	4
	Sliced cheese, sliced tomatoes and lettuce, optional	

1. In a food processor, combine tofu, potatoes, garlic, onion, oats, flour, soy sauce, tahini and mustard. Pulse until mixture is finely ground and holds together. Transfer to a bowl and stir in sunflower seeds. With moistened hands, shape into 4 patties, about 3/4 inch (2 cm) thick.

2. In a large skillet, heat oil over medium heat. Fry patties, turning once, for about 5 minutes per side or until hot in the center and well browned.

3. Serve in a buns topped with cheese, tomatoes and lettuce as desired.

Cheese Fondue

A treat to linger over with a loved one or close friends. Taking time to savor this is a must.

Serves 4

Tip

Vacherin des Bois Francs is an artisan cheese from Quebec, Canada. This semifirm, washed-rind cheese is a good melting cheese. Other Vacherin varieties from France and Switzerland are available. Look for them at specialty cheese shops. If you have difficultly finding Vacherin, Gruyère is a good substitute in this recipe.

- **Preheat oven to 400°F (200°C)**
- **Cheese fondue pot with burner**

1	baguette, cut into 1-inch (2.5 cm) cubes	1
2 tsp	olive oil	10 mL
1/4 cup	finely chopped French shallots	60 mL
2	cloves garlic, finely chopped	2
1 cup	white wine	250 mL
2 1/2 cups	shredded Vacherin des Bois Francs or Gruyère cheese (see Tip, left)	625 mL
2 1/2 cups	shredded Emmental or other Swiss cheese	625 mL
1/2 tsp	paprika	2 mL

1. Spread bread cubes on a baking sheet and toast in preheated oven for about 5 minutes or until starting to brown.

2. Meanwhile, in a cheese fondue pot or a saucepan, heat oil over medium heat. Sauté shallots and garlic for about 5 minutes or until very soft. Pour in wine and bring to a boil. Boil until slightly reduced. Reduce heat to low and gradually stir in Vacherin and Emmental cheeses, one handful at a time, making sure the first addition is almost melted before adding the next. Stir in paprika.

3. Place fondue pot over a fondue flame and serve with toasted bread cubes for dipping.

Sweet Potato Shepherd's Pie

Sweet potatoes and tofu completely transform this great classic for the better.

Serves 4 to 6

- **Preheat oven to 350°F (180°C)**
- **8-inch (20 cm) square glass baking dish, greased**
- **Food processor**

2 cups	cubed sweet potatoes (about 1 large)	500 mL
	Salt	
1 tbsp	olive oil	15 mL
1	clove garlic, chopped	1
1	onion, chopped	1
1	zucchini, grated	1
8 oz	firm tofu, crumbled	250 g
¼ cup	tamari (see Tip, page 126)	60 mL
1 tsp	ground coriander	5 mL
2 cups	frozen corn kernels	500 mL
¼ cup	milk	60 mL

1. Place sweet potatoes in a saucepan and add enough cold water to cover by 1 inch (2.5 cm). Bring to a boil and season with salt to taste. Reduce heat and simmer for 10 to 15 minutes or until tender. Drain well.

2. Meanwhile, in a skillet, heat oil over medium heat. Sauté garlic, onion, zucchini and tofu for about 8 minutes or until onion is softened. Stir in tamari and coriander and sauté for 3 to 5 minutes or until vegetables are browned. Place in prepared baking dish. Spread corn evenly over top.

3. In a food processor, purée sweet potatoes with milk until smooth. Spread mixture on top of corn.

4. Bake in preheated oven for about 30 minutes or until hot and topping starts to brown.

Polenta Mountain

The presentation of this recipe is a peak experience that never fails to attract attention.

Makes 6 polenta mountains

Tip
Be sure to use a fine cornmeal to ensure it cooks quickly.

• **6- or 12-cup muffin pan, 6 cups greased**

4 cups	water	1 L
Pinch	salt	Pinch
1 cup	fine yellow cornmeal (see Tip, left)	250 mL
2 tbsp	olive oil, divided	30 mL
½	onion, chopped	½
1	clove garlic, chopped	1
1	carrot, chopped	1
½	zucchini, chopped	½
10	olives, chopped	10
5	stalks asparagus, chopped	5
5	leaves spinach, trimmed and chopped	5
1	can (14 oz/398 mL) plum (Roma) tomatoes	1
1 tsp	dried oregano	5 mL
	Salt and freshly ground black pepper	

1. In a pot, bring water and salt to a boil over high heat. Gradually pour in cornmeal, stirring constantly. Boil, stirring, for about 5 minutes or until cornmeal is softened and thick. Spoon into prepared muffin cups. Let cool.

2. Meanwhile, in a skillet, heat 1 tbsp (15 mL) of the oil over medium heat. Sauté onion and garlic for about 5 minutes or until softened. Add carrot, zucchini, olives, asparagus and spinach and sauté for about 5 minutes or until carrots start to soften. Stir in tomatoes and oregano. Reduce heat and simmer for about 15 minutes or until vegetables are tender. Season with salt and pepper to taste.

Tips

If you have silicone muffin liners or silicone muffin pans, they make removal of the polenta muffins even easier.

Feel free to change-up the vegetables according to your preferences and what's in season. Just substitute approximately the same amount to make sure there is enough sauce.

3. Meanwhile, preheat broiler.

4. To serve, cut polenta muffins in half crosswise and place on a baking sheet. Brush with remaining oil. Broil for about 3 minutes or until starting to brown. Divide about two-thirds of the sauce equally among 6 serving plates. Place muffin bottom over sauce. Add more sauce over bottom half and cover with remaining muffin top.

Variation

Polenta Mountains Arrabbiata: Add a pinch of hot pepper flakes with the salt when cooking the polenta. Add 1 finely chopped red hot chile pepper with the carrots and increase the garlic to 3 to 4 cloves, or to taste.

Vegetarian Chop Suey

Leave the bean sprouts a little crunchy for the best flavor and texture.

Serves 2 to 4

1 tbsp	olive oil	15 mL
4	green onions, sliced	4
1	zucchini, julienned	1
8 oz	extra-firm or firm tofu, julienned	250 g
12	mushrooms, sliced	12
3 tbsp	tamari	45 mL
2 tbsp	freshly grated Parmesan cheese	30 mL
½ tsp	hot pepper sauce	2 mL
3 cups	bean sprouts (see Tip, left)	750 mL
	Salt and freshly ground black pepper	

Tip

The bean sprout is a mungo bean that looks like a tiny green bean, but after it germinates in water, it turns into a tasty sprout.

1. In a large skillet or a wok, heat oil over medium–high heat. Stir-fry green onions for 3 minutes or until softened.

2. Add zucchini, tofu and mushrooms and stir-fry for about 5 minutes or until mushrooms start to brown. Stir in tamari, Parmesan cheese and hot pepper sauce. Add bean sprouts and stir-fry for 2 minutes or until slightly wilted. Season with salt and pepper to taste.

Vegetable Paella

In 30 minutes you'll enjoy the magnificent aroma of this vegetable paella.

Serves 4

Tips

A classic dish from the Valencia region of Spain, paella is perfect for parties. Originally it contained vegetables, meat and snails, and was cooked slowly over glowing embers. Now there are many versions — seafood paella is perhaps the most popular — but all display the distinctive color of saffron.

If you prefer, you can peel the tomatoes before dicing them. Plunge the tomatoes into a pot of boiling water for 1 minute. Immediately transfer to a bowl of ice water to chill, then peel off skins.

1 tbsp	olive oil	15 mL
1	clove garlic, chopped	1
1/2	Spanish onion, chopped	1/2
20	fresh green beans	20
1	carrot, diced	1
1/2 cup	drained rinsed canned white beans	125 mL
1/2 cup	frozen green peas	125 mL
15	leaves spinach, trimmed	15
2	tomatoes, diced (see Tips, left)	2
1 cup	long-grain white rice	250 mL
2 cups	vegetable broth	500 mL
1/2 tsp	paprika	2 mL
Pinch	saffron threads	Pinch

1. In a large skillet, heat oil over medium heat. Sauté garlic and onion for about 5 minutes or until softened. Add green beans, carrot, white beans, peas, spinach and tomatoes and sauté for about 5 minutes or until carrots start to soften.

2. Stir in rice, broth, paprika and saffron and bring to a boil. Reduce heat and simmer gently, without stirring, for 15 to 20 minutes or until rice is tender and most of liquid has been absorbed. At the end of cooking, you can remove the pan from the heat and cover the paella with a damp cloth for a few minutes to allow the flavors to really blend together.

Stuffed Squash

This recipe is at its glory in the fall, when the squash are ready for harvest and an oven-roasted meal warms both body and soul.

Serves 2 to 4

Tip
Choose a nice, large squash that feels heavy for its size.

- Preheat oven to 400°F (200°C)
- 13- by 9-inch (33 by 23 cm) glass baking dish

1	butternut or acorn squash (see Tip, left)	1
2 tbsp	butter	30 mL
1 tbsp	olive oil	15 mL
1	clove garlic, chopped	1
$\frac{1}{2}$	onion, chopped	$\frac{1}{2}$
2 cups	diced zucchini	500 mL
2 cups	sliced mushrooms	500 mL
6 tbsp	light sour cream	90 mL
1 tbsp	Dijon mustard	15 mL
1 cup	shredded Cheddar cheese	250 mL
	Paprika	

1. Cut squash in half lengthwise. Scoop out seeds and place, cut side up, in baking dish. Divide butter equally in each cavity. Bake in preheated oven for about 40 minutes or until squash is tender.

2. Meanwhile, in a skillet, heat oil over medium–high heat. Sauté garlic, onion, zucchini and mushrooms for about 8 minutes or until mushrooms are browned. Remove from heat and stir in sour cream and mustard.

3. Spoon vegetables into hollow of squash and top with cheese. Garnish with paprika and bake in preheated oven for about 5 minutes or until cheese is melted.

Stuffed Peppers

A perfect pick for fall, this recipe will help you rediscover the rich sweetness and fine flavor of red peppers.

Serves 4

Tip

One 14-oz (398 mL) can of lentils yields about 1½ cups (375 mL). If you have a larger can, you can refrigerate the extra lentils in an airtight container for up to 2 days or freezer for up to 3 months.

- **Preheat oven to 300°F (150°C)**
- **8-cup (2 L) shallow glass baking dish or casserole dish**

2	large red bell peppers	2
1 tbsp	olive oil	15 mL
1	clove garlic, chopped	1
½	red onion, chopped	½
2	plum (Roma) tomatoes, diced	2
1½ cups	drained rinsed canned lentils (see Tip, left)	375 mL
⅓ cup	creamy goat cheese	75 mL
	Salt and freshly ground black pepper	

1. Cut bell peppers in half lengthwise. Remove the core and seeds, leaving stems intact.

2. In a large pot of boiling water, blanch peppers for 3 minutes. Drain well and set aside.

3. In a skillet, heat oil over medium heat. Sauté garlic and red onion for about 5 minutes or until softened. Stir in tomatoes, lentils and goat cheese. Season with salt and pepper to taste.

4. Spoon filling into peppers. Place in baking dish. Bake in preheated oven for about 20 minutes or until peppers are tender and filling is hot.

Asparagus in Vinaigrette
and Lemony Artichokes

Sides

Here's an amazing array of recipes for vegetables, potatoes and rice to accompany your main dishes. You'll see that these sides are just as dazzling, colorful and inviting as the rest of the food on the plate. They may even become the focus of your meals.

Asparagus in Vinaigrette 140

Lemony Artichokes 141

Beans with Tomatoes 142

Fragrant Carrots 143

Cauliflower with Curry 144

Broccoli in Creamy Sauce 145

Patatas Bravas 146

Sweet Potato Muffins 147

Swiss Chard Gratin 148

Potatoes with Swiss Chard 149

Stuffed Zucchini 150

Eggplant with Tomato 151

Oven-Roasted Vegetables 152

Two-Color Potatoes 153

Basmati Rice with Peas
    and Nuts 154

Rice with Cranberries
    and Curry 155

Asparagus in Vinaigrette

This recipe will make you appreciate the arrival of spring even more. If your asparagus spears are small, use about 40.

Serves 4

Tip

Choose firm spears of asparagus with tightly closed leaves on top. Any sign of wrinkling or the leaves spreading means it's past its prime.

Steamer basket

30	spears asparagus (see Tip, left)	30
1 tbsp	sesame seeds	15 mL

Vinaigrette

2 tbsp	olive oil	30 mL
1 tbsp	white wine vinegar	15 mL
1 tbsp	balsamic vinegar	15 mL
1 tsp	Dijon mustard	5 mL
1 tsp	pure maple syrup	5 mL
Pinch	herbes de Provence	Pinch
	Salt and freshly ground black pepper	

1. Break off the tough ends of the asparagus and discard. In a steamer basket set in a pot of boiling water, steam asparagus for 2 to 3 minutes or until bright green and slightly crunchy. Transfer to a serving bowl.

2. Meanwhile, in a small, dry skillet over medium heat, toast sesame seeds, stirring constantly, for about 3 minutes or until golden and fragrant. Immediately transfer to a bowl.

3. *Vinaigrette:* In a small bowl or measuring cup, whisk together oil, white wine vinegar, balsamic vinegar, mustard, maple syrup and herbes de Provence. Season with salt and pepper to taste. Pour over asparagus. Sprinkle toasted sesame seeds on top.

Lemony Artichokes

Here is a really simple recipe that adds a touch of lemon to accompany your main dish.

Serves 4 to 6

Tip

Some people claim that the artichoke has aphrodisiacal properties. Its main appeal, however, is its exquisite, tender heart, which is found in cans making them perfect for this quick side dish.

2 tbsp	olive oil	30 mL
2	cans (each 14 oz/ 398 mL) artichoke hearts, drained and cut into pieces (see Tip, left)	2
2	cloves garlic, chopped	2
¼ cup	fresh parsley leaves, chopped	60 mL
2 tbsp	freshly squeezed lemon juice	30 mL
2 tsp	Dijon mustard	10 mL
	Salt and freshly ground black pepper	

1. In a skillet, heat oil over medium heat. Add artichokes and garlic and sauté for about 5 minutes or until hot. Stir in parsley, lemon juice and mustard. Season with salt and pepper to taste.

Beans with Tomatoes

These green beans will disappear in no time.

Serves 4

Tip
When yellow (wax) beans are in season, try a mixture with the green for an added splash of color.

1 tbsp	olive oil	15 mL
1	clove garlic, chopped	1
1	onion, chopped	1
2	tomatoes, diced	2
6 cups	green beans, trimmed (see Tip, left)	1.5 L
1 tsp	dried oregano	5 mL
	Salt and freshly ground black pepper	

1. In a pot, heat oil over medium heat. Sauté garlic and onion for about 5 minutes or until softened. Add tomatoes and let simmer for about 5 minutes or until softened and juices are released.

2. Stir in green beans and oregano. Reduce heat and simmer, stirring often, for about 5 minutes or until beans are tender-crisp. Season with salt and pepper to taste.

Fragrant Carrots

This recipe intensifies the sweet smell and taste of the carrots.

Serves 4

Tip

If you can find heirloom carrots in different colors (yellow, white, purple, red), this is a terrific recipe to highlight their unusual look and delicious flavor.

• **Steamer basket**

3 cups	julienned carrots (see Tip, left)	750 mL
1 tbsp	olive oil	15 mL
1	clove garlic, chopped	1
¼ tsp	ground cumin	1 mL
1 tsp	liquid honey	5 mL
	Salt and freshly ground black pepper	

1. In a steamer basket set in a pot of boiling water, steam carrots for 5 to 7 minutes or until tender-crisp.

2. In a skillet, heat oil over medium heat. Sauté garlic for about 2 minutes or until softened. Stir in carrots, cumin and honey and sauté for about 3 minutes or until carrots are coated and tender. Season with salt and pepper to taste.

Cauliflower with Curry

Curry adds an exotic touch to the cauliflower, creating a dish which is the perfect companion to a quiche or omelet.

Serves 4

Tip

If you prefer, you can cook the sauce in the microwave.

• **Steamer basket**

1	large cauliflower, cut into florets	1
2 tbsp	butter	30 mL
2 tbsp	all-purpose flour	30 mL
½ tsp	curry powder	2 mL
1¼ cups	milk	300 mL
1 tsp	salt	5 mL
	Freshly ground black pepper	

1. In a steamer basket set in a pot of boiling water, steam cauliflower for about 10 minutes or until tender.

2. In a small saucepan, melt butter over medium heat. Sprinkle with flour and curry powder and cook, stirring, for 1 minute. Gradually whisk in milk. Bring to a simmer, whisking constantly. Reduce heat and simmer, stirring, for about 3 minutes or until sauce has thickened. Stir in salt and season with pepper to taste.

3. Transfer cauliflower to a serving bowl and pour sauce on top.

Broccoli in Creamy Sauce

Broccoli is good all by itself, but this light sauce enhances its flavor.

Serves 4

Tip

You can save on preparation time by buying precut broccoli florets, often found in bags or loose in the produce department of supermarkets. Use 1 lb (500 g) florets for this recipe.

• **Steamer basket**

1	small bunch broccoli, cut into florets	1
1 tbsp	freshly grated Parmesan cheese	15 mL
¼ cup	cottage cheese	60 mL
1 tbsp	olive oil	15 mL
1 tbsp	apple cider vinegar	15 mL
1 tsp	Dijon mustard	5 mL
	Salt and freshly ground black pepper	

1. In a steamer basket set in a pot of boiling water, steam broccoli for about 8 minutes or until tender-crisp.

2. Meanwhile, in a blender or using an immersion blender in a cup, purée Parmesan cheese, cottage cheese, oil, vinegar and mustard until smooth. Season with salt and pepper to taste. Transfer broccoli to a serving bowl and pour sauce on top.

Patatas Bravas

A great classic in Spanish cuisine, this dish delivers a spicy flavor that is out of the ordinary.

Serves 4

Tip

Patatas bravas bars often serve them as tapas. Using high-quality mayonnaise takes these tapas over the top.

- **Preheat oven to 400°F (200°C)**
- **Rimmed baking sheet**

7 cups	cubed potatoes	1.75 L
2 tbsp	olive oil	30 mL
1 tsp	salt	5 mL
3 tbsp	mayonnaise	45 mL
12	drops hot pepper sauce	12

1. In a bowl, cover potatoes with warm water and let soak for 10 minutes. Drain and dry thoroughly with a clean, lint-free towel.

2. In a large bowl, combine potatoes, oil and salt, tossing to coat well.

3. Spread potato mixture in a single layer on baking sheet. Bake in preheated oven for about 50 minutes, stirring every 10 minutes.

4. Return potatoes to the bowl, add mayonnaise and hot pepper sauce and toss gently to coat. Serve immediately.

Sweet Potato Muffins

These muffins are crispy on the outside and soft on the inside.

Makes 9 muffins

• Preheat oven to 400°F (200°C)
• 12-cup muffin pan, 9 cups greased

Tip

There is often confusion about sweet potatoes and yams. For this recipe, you want the sweet, orange-fleshed potatoes with a reddish skin. Though they're often labeled "yams" at the supermarket, they are, in fact, sweet potatoes. True yams have a brown skin, white flesh and a starchy texture and aren't as sweet and flavorful.

1½ cups	all-purpose flour	375 mL
½ cup	cornstarch	125 mL
1 tbsp	baking powder	15 mL
½ tsp	salt	2 mL
1 cup	grated sweet potato (see Tip, left)	250 mL
½	zucchini, grated	½
½ cup	chopped onion	125 mL
½ cup	finely diced Swiss cheese	125 mL
1	clove garlic, chopped	1
2	eggs	2
¾ cup	milk	175 mL
¼ cup	melted butter	60 mL
1 tsp	Dijon mustard	5 mL
Pinch	cayenne pepper	Pinch

1. In a large bowl, combine flour, cornstarch, baking powder and salt. Stir in sweet potato, zucchini, onion, Swiss cheese and garlic.

2. In another bowl, whisk together eggs, milk, butter, mustard and cayenne. Pour over dry ingredients and stir just until moistened.

3. Spoon into prepared muffin cups. Bake in preheated oven for about 20 minutes or until tops spring back when lightly touched. Serve hot or transfer to a rack and let cool completely.

Swiss Chard Gratin

With a hearty flavor that's similar to spinach, Swiss chard has a lot of character.

Serves 4 to 6

Tip

Swiss chard comes in a variety of colors. Look for red, yellow and white and use a mixture for a very attractive dish.

- **Preheat broiler**
- **Steamer basket**
- **4-cup (1 L) shallow baking dish**

15	leaves Swiss chard, tough ends trimmed off (see Tip, left)	15
1 cup	shredded Gruyère or Emmental cheese	250 mL
	Paprika	

1. In a steamer basket set in a pot of boiling water, steam Swiss chard leaves for 5 to 10 minutes or until tender. Drain well. Place in a baking dish.

2. Sprinkle with cheese and paprika. Broil for about 3 minutes or until cheese is melted and starting to brown.

Variation

You can substitute kale for the Swiss chard, just increase the cooking time in Step 1 to 10 to 15 minutes.

Potatoes with Swiss Chard

This recipe was inspired by Spanish cuisine.

Serves 4

Tip

Choose a waxy white or red-skinned potato or an all-purpose yellow-fleshed one for this recipe so they hold their shape. Baking potatoes will become crumbly.

1 tbsp	olive oil	15 mL
1	clove garlic, chopped	1
4	potatoes, diced (see Tip, left)	4
1 cup	chopped Swiss chard stems	250 mL
1 cup	water	250 mL
2 tsp	white wine vinegar or red wine vinegar	10 mL
	Salt and freshly ground black pepper	

1. In a large pot, heat oil over medium heat. Sauté garlic for about 3 minutes or until golden.

2. Add potatoes and sauté for 5 minutes or until starting to soften. Add Swiss chard and water. Boil, shaking the pot occasionally, for about 10 minutes or until potatoes are tender and browned.

3. Stir in vinegar and season with salt and pepper to taste.

Stuffed Zucchini

These delicious little zucchini "boats" sailed smoothly into my family's list of favorite foods.

Serves 4

Tip
Choose medium-large zucchini for this recipe. If they're too small, there won't be enough room for the filling.

- **Preheat oven to 400°F (200°C)**
- **13- by 9-inch (33 by 23 cm) glass baking dish**

4	zucchini (see Tip, left)	4
1 tsp	olive oil	5 mL
2	French shallots, chopped	2
1	clove garlic, chopped	1
1	carrot, diced	1
¼ tsp	dried savory	1 mL
½ cup	drained rinsed canned chickpeas	125 mL
2	plum (Roma) tomatoes, diced	2
	Salt and freshly ground black pepper	
1	egg	1
1 cup	shredded sharp (aged) Cheddar cheese	250 mL
Pinch	paprika	Pinch

1. Cut zucchini in half lengthwise. Using a small spoon, scoop out the flesh of the zucchini leaving ¼ inch (0.5 cm) walls (reserve flesh for another use, if desired).

2. In a pot of boiling water, blanch zucchini for 2 minutes. Drain well and set aside.

3. In a skillet, heat oil over medium heat. Sauté shallots, garlic, carrot and savory for about 8 minutes or until tender. Stir in chickpeas and tomatoes and season with salt and pepper to taste. Remove from heat and stir in egg.

4. Spoon filling into zucchini. Place in baking dish and sprinkle with cheese and paprika. Bake in preheated oven for 5 to 10 minutes or until filling is hot and cheese is melted.

Eggplant with Tomato

Prepare and serve this recipe in individual portions, to let each one really shine. Accompanied by a salad, this dish can become the star of your meal.

Serves 4

• Preheat oven to 400°F (200°C)

• Preheat oven to 400°F (200°C)
• Four ovenproof plates (see Tip, left)

1	eggplant	1
2 tbsp	olive oil, divided	30 mL
	Salt	
2	zucchini	2
3	plum (Roma) tomatoes	3
12	slices mozzarella cheese	12
	Dried oregano	

Tip

If you don't have ovenproof plates, build these stacks on small squares of parchment paper or foil on a baking sheet. Bake them and carefully transfer the paper to serving plates, then slide the paper from under the stack, holding the stack in place on the plate with a spatula.

1. Cut eggplant crosswise into 12 slices. Place on a baking sheet, brush both sides with half of the oil and sprinkle with salt to taste.

2. Bake in preheated oven for about 15 minutes or until tender and lightly browned.

3. Meanwhile, peel zucchini and cut into small dice. In a skillet, heat remaining oil over medium-high heat. Sauté zucchini for about 3 minutes or until just tender. Remove from heat.

4. Cut tomatoes crosswise into 8 slices each.

5. On each of 4 plates, place 1 slice of eggplant in the center. Top each with 1 slice of cheese, then 2 slices of tomato. Sprinkle tomato with oregano to taste. Top each with another slice of eggplant and spoon zucchini mixture equally over each. Top with 1 slice of cheese and 2 slices of tomato. Sprinkle with oregano. Repeat once more with eggplant, cheese and tomato. Bake in preheated oven for 5 to 10 minutes or until hot.

Oven-Roasted Vegetables

True delights, these roasted veggies are irresistible.

Serves 4

Tip
Cut the vegetables lengthwise into large pieces, so they're all the same size.

• **Preheat oven to 450°F (230°C)**

½	butternut squash (see Tip, left)	½
1	sweet potato	1
2	carrots	2
2	parsnips	3
¼	rutabaga	¼
½	Spanish onion, cut into wedges	½
1	clove garlic, minced	1
3 tbsp	olive oil	45 mL
1 tsp	dried oregano	5 mL
½ tsp	salt	2 mL
½ tsp	paprika	2 mL

1. Peel squash, sweet potatoes, carrots, parsnips and rutabaga and cut into sticks about 3 inches (7.5 cm) long by ½ inch (1 cm) thick. Place in a bowl and add lukewarm water to cover. Let stand for 10 minutes. Drain and pat dry with a clean, lint-free towel and return to dry bowl.

2. Add onion wedges, garlic, oil, oregano, salt and paprika and toss to coat. Spread vegetables in a single layer on a large baking sheet. Bake in preheated oven for about 50 minutes, turning pieces every 10 minutes, or until browned and tender.

Two-Color Potatoes

These spuds add a dash of color to your main dish.

Serves 4

Tip

You can also sprinkle the top of the baked dish with shredded Cheddar cheese and broil to brown to make an au gratin dish.

- **Preheat oven to 400°F (200°C)**
- **8-cup (2 L) shallow baking dish, greased**

3 cups	sliced peeled sweet potatoes	750 mL
3 cups	sliced peeled potatoes	750 mL
1 tbsp	butter	15 mL
2	cloves garlic, chopped	2
1	onion, chopped	1
1¾ cups	milk	425 mL
1 tsp	salt	5 mL
¼ tsp	ground nutmeg	1 mL
	Freshly ground black pepper	

1. Rinse sweet potatoes and potatoes under running water. Drain well and pat dry with a clean, lint-free towel.

2. In a large skillet, melt butter over medium heat. Sauté garlic and onion for about 5 minutes or until softened. Add sweet potatoes, potatoes, milk, salt, nutmeg, and pepper to taste. Reduce heat and simmer, shaking pan occasionally, for about 15 minutes or until potatoes start to soften.

3. Spread in prepared baking dish. Bake in preheated oven for about 30 minutes or until potatoes are tender and top is browned.

Basmati Rice with Peas and Nuts

The combination of tender, juicy peas and rich nuts adds texture, color and flavor to the basmati rice.

Serves 4

Tip

If you don't have an ovenproof skillet with a lid, pour the rice mixture into a 4-cup (1 L) baking dish after Step 1 and add about 5 minutes to the baking time.

- **Preheat oven to at 400°F (200°C)**
- **Ovenproof skillet with lid (see Tip, left)**

1 tbsp	olive oil	15 mL
1	clove garlic, chopped	1
½	onion, chopped	½
1 cup	basmati rice	250 mL
1½ cups	water	375 mL
¼ cup	milk	60 mL
Pinch	granulated sugar	Pinch
¾ cup	frozen green peas, thawed	175 mL
¾ cup	mixed slivered cashews and almonds	175 mL

1. In a skillet, heat oil over medium heat. Sauté garlic and onion for about 5 minutes or until softened. Stir in rice and sauté for 1 minute. Stir in water, milk, sugar and peas and bring to a simmer.

2. Cover and bake in preheated oven for about 20 minutes or until the liquid has been absorbed. Let stand, covered, for 5 minutes. Fluff with a fork. Transfer to a serving bowl.

3. Meanwhile, in a small, dry skillet over medium, heat, toast cashews and almonds, stirring constantly, for about 5 minutes or until golden and fragrant. Sprinkle over rice.

Rice with Cranberries and Curry

This colorful rice dish serves up an explosion of salty-sweet flavor.

Serves 4

Tip

Native to North American bogs, cranberry vines produce the bright, tart fruit that is a perennial favorite beside festive roast turkey. Dried cranberries are ever more popular as a healthy snack on their own, or as colorful additions to everyday dishes ranging from porridge to salads to baked goods.

• **6-cup (1.5 L) microwave-safe glass dish**

1 cup	basmati rice	250 mL
2 cups	vegetable broth	500 mL
2 tbsp	dried cranberries	30 mL
1 tbsp	olive oil	15 mL
1	onion, chopped	1
1	carrot, diced	1
½	red bell pepper, finely chopped	½
2 tbsp	sunflower seeds	30 mL
1 tsp	granulated sugar	5 mL
½ tsp	curry powder	2 mL

1. In a microwave-safe dish, combine rice, vegetable broth and cranberries. Cover (leaving one corner vented, if using plastic wrap) and microwave on High, stirring twice, for 12 to 15 minutes or until tender. Let stand, covered, for 5 minutes.

2. Meanwhile, in a skillet, heat oil over medium heat. Sauté onion and carrot for about 5 minutes or until softened. Add bell pepper, sunflower seeds, sugar and curry and sauté for about 5 minutes or until peppers are tender. Using a fork, gently stir into rice.

Ricotta Coconut Cake

Desserts

To satisfy everyone's secret sweet tooth, the following pages serve up delicious pleasures, healthy treats your children will love and desserts that are truly decadent (which is just the way we want them). Occasional indulgence can't hurt.

Banana Honey Fritters. 158

Fruit with Cream 159

Fruit Parfait 160

Three-Fruit Salad. 161

Apple Delight 162

Apple Crisp 163

Strawberry Mounds 164

Strawberry Rhubarb Crumble 165

Pineapple Muffins. 166

Blueberry Muffins 168

Banana Muffins. 169

Apple Muffins 170

Oatmeal Cookies. 171

Chocolate Chip Cookies 172

Peanut Butter Cookies. 173

Granola Bars 174

Date Mini-Bites. 175

Date Squares. 176

Grandmother's Sugar Pie 177

Lemon Pie 178

Ricotta Coconut Cake 180

Creamy Fruit Delight. 181

Banana Honey Fritters

Inspired by Asian sweets, here's an especially nice dessert to enjoy after a light meal.

Serves 4

Tip
Use bananas that are just ripe but still firm. If they're too soft they'll become very mushy when fried.

4	firm bananas (see Tip, left)	4
	Vegetable oil	
¼ cup	all-purpose flour (approx.)	60 mL
2	eggs	2
2 tbsp	liquid honey, heated	30 mL
2 tbsp	sesame seeds	30 mL

1. Cut bananas in half lengthwise. Without separating the two halves, cut crosswise into about 8 slices.

2. In a large, deep skillet, heat 2 inches (5 cm) of oil over medium heat until hot, but not smoking.

3. Meanwhile, place flour in a bowl. In a shallow dish, whisk eggs until blended. Dip banana pieces first in flour to coat, shaking off excess, then dip in egg. Place on a baking sheet. Discard any excess flour and egg.

4. Fry 5 or 6 banana pieces at a time in hot oil, turning once, for about 4 minutes or until golden. Place on a clean baking sheet, lined with paper towel to dry. Adjust heat in between batches as necessary to prevent burning.

5. Dip hot banana pieces in honey and then in sesame seeds. Serve immediately.

Fruit with Cream

I know people who would walk a mile for even a little bowl of this fruit with cream. This recipe really brings out the best in fresh fruit.

Serves 4

Tip

Use a combination of cubed honeydew melon, sliced strawberries and red grapes or cherries.

2 tbsp	butter	30 mL
2 tbsp	all-purpose flour	30 mL
1 cup	half-and-half (10%) or table (18%) cream	250 mL
1/3 cup	granulated sugar	75 mL
1/2 tsp	vanilla extract	2 mL
4 cups	bite-size pieces fresh fruit (see Tip, left)	1 L

1. In a saucepan, melt butter over medium-low heat. In a measuring cup, whisk flour into cream. Gradually pour into saucepan, while whisking. Increase heat to medium and bring to a boil, whisking constantly. Boil, whisking, for about 3 minutes or until thickened. Stir in sugar and vanilla. Remove from heat.

2. Stir in fruit and let cool until just warm.

Fruit Parfait

Here's a light dessert you can serve in individual fruit cups — in summer or winter. It's great with fresh fruit when it's in season, and just as good with frozen or canned.

Serves 4

• 4 parfait glasses or serving bowls		
½ cup	blueberries	125 mL
2 cups	vanilla-flavored yogurt	500 mL
4	slices pineapple, chopped	4
½ cup	sliced strawberries	125 mL

1. Place one-quarter of the blueberries in each glass.

2. Top each with ¼ cup (60 mL) yogurt, one-quarter of the pineapple, ¼ cup (60 mL) yogurt, then one-quarter of the strawberries.

Variation

Peach Melba Parfait: Replace the blueberries and strawberries with raspberries and replace the pineapple with 2 sliced peaches.

> **Tip**
>
> If you use frozen fruits, let them thaw at room temperature or defrost in the microwave before preparing the dessert. Drain off any excess liquid.

Patatas Bravas (page 146) and
Sweet Potato Muffins (page 147)

Swiss Chard Gratin (page 148) and
Potatoes with Swiss Chard (page 149)

Oven-Roasted Vegetables (page 152)

Basmati Rice with Peas and Nuts (page 154),
Rice with Cranberries and Curry (page 155)
and Risotto with Sun-Dried Tomatoes (page 85)

Fruit with Cream (page 159),
Fruit Parfait (page 160) and
Three-Fruit Salad (page 161)

Strawberry Rhubarb Crumble (page 165)
and Strawberry Mounds (page 164)

Pineapple Muffins (page 166), Blueberry Muffins (page 168), Banana Muffins (page 169) and Apple Muffins (page 170)

Grandmother's Sugar Pie (page 177)

Three-Fruit Salad

Lemon juice adds a fresh personality to this fruit salad.

Serves 4

Tip

Honeydew melon is related to gourds and cucumbers. To select a melon that is ripe, choose one that feels heavy for its size and smells sweet.

2 cups	cubed pineapple	500 mL
2 cups	cubed watermelon	500 mL
2 cups	cubed honeydew melon (see Tip, left)	500 mL
3 tbsp	freshly squeezed lemon juice	45 mL

1. In a large bowl, combine pineapple, watermelon and honeydew. Squeeze lemon juice on top.

2. Let stand for 10 minutes to allow flavors to blend before serving.

Variation

Honey Ginger Three-Fruit Salad: In a small saucepan, combine 2 tbsp (30 mL) liquid honey, $\frac{1}{2}$ tsp (2 mL) minced gingerroot and the lemon juice. Heat over low heat, stirring, until ginger is softened and mixture is fragrant. Pour over the fruit in Step 1.

Apple Delight

When apples are in season, everyone looks for new apple dessert recipes. Contrary to the Apple Crisp (page 163), this dessert shows off its apples on the top.

Serves 4

(page 163)

Tip

Choose cooking apples that hold their shape and flavor when baked, such as Cortland, Granny Smith, Crispin (Mutsu), Northern Spy or Empire.

- **Preheat oven to 350°F (180°C)**
- **8-inch (20 cm) square metal baking pan, lightly greased**

1⅓ cups	all-purpose flour	325 mL
½ cup	granulated sugar	125 mL
1 tbsp	baking powder	15 mL
Pinch	salt	Pinch
¼ cup	cold butter, cut into thin slices	60 mL
1	egg, beaten	1
¾ cup	milk	175 mL

Topping

4	cooking apples, peeled and sliced (see Tip, left)	4
2 tbsp	granulated sugar	30 mL
½ tsp	ground cinnamon	2 mL
¼ tsp	ground nutmeg	1 mL

1. In a large bowl, combine flour, sugar, baking powder and salt. Using a pastry blender or two knives, cut in butter until mixture resembles fine crumbs. Using a fork, stir in egg and milk to make a soft, sticky dough. Place dough in prepared baking pan.

2. *Topping:* Spread apple slices on top. Sprinkle with sugar, cinnamon and nutmeg.

3. Bake in preheated oven for about 40 minutes or until apples are tender and a tester inserted into cake portion comes out clean.

Apple Crisp

Feel free to reduce the amount of brown sugar if you prefer a crisp that is less sweet.

Serves 4 to 6

Tip

Apples have been cultivated for about 3,000 years, and now there are almost more varieties than we can count. For cooking, choose an apple, such as Cortland, that stays firm. Other good choices are Granny Smith, Crispin (Mutsu), Northern Spy or Empire.

- **Preheat oven to 350°F (180°C)**
- **8-inch (20 cm) square glass baking dish, greased**

1 cup	all-purpose flour	250 mL
1 cup	quick-cooking rolled oats	250 mL
¾ cup	packed brown sugar	175 mL
1 tsp	ground cinnamon	5 mL
½ cup	melted butter	125 mL
5 cups	peeled sliced apples, such as Cortland (see Tip, left)	1.25 L

1. In a bowl, combine flour, oats, brown sugar, cinnamon and melted butter. Place apples in a large bowl and add one-quarter of the oat mixture and toss gently to coat. Spread in prepared baking dish. Sprinkle remaining oat mixture evenly on top.

2. Bake in preheated oven for about 30 minutes or until apples are tender and topping is golden and crisp.

Variations

Apple Cherry Crisp: Add ½ cup (125 mL) dried sour cherries with the apples.

Apple Cranberry Crisp: Reduce the apples to 4 cups (1 L) and add 1 cup (250 mL) fresh or frozen cranberries, or keep apples at 5 cups (1.25 L) and add ½ cup (125 mL) dried cranberries.

Strawberry Mounds

Fruit desserts are always popular, and strawberries win unanimous approval.

Serves 4 to 6

Tip
You can make this four-season recipe with frozen strawberries when fresh aren't in season or any other berries.

- **Preheat oven to 400°F (200°C)**
- **6-cup (1.5 L) rectangular or oval glass or ceramic baking dish**

2½ cups	thickly sliced strawberries (see Tip, left)	625 mL
¼ cup	granulated sugar	60 mL
2 tbsp	all-purpose flour	30 mL
¾ cup	water	175 mL

Topping

1 cup	all-purpose flour	250 mL
1 tbsp	granulated sugar	15 mL
2 tsp	baking powder	10 mL
¼ tsp	salt	1 mL
3 tbsp	cold butter, cut into thin slices	45 mL
1	egg, beaten	1
⅓ cup	milk	75 mL

1. In a microwave-safe bowl, combine strawberries, sugar, flour and water. Microwave on High, stirring every 2 minutes, for 7 to 8 minutes or until thickened. Transfer to a rectangular baking dish.

2. *Topping:* In a bowl, mix flour with sugar, baking powder and salt. Using a pastry blender or two knives, cut in butter until mixture resembles fine crumbs. Using a fork, stir in egg and milk to make a soft, sticky dough.

3. Using a spoon, scoop about 8 balls of dough and place on top of the strawberries.

4. Bake in preheated oven for about 20 minutes or until topping is golden and a tester inserted in the center comes out clean. Let cool slightly in dish on a wire rack. Serve warm.

Strawberry Rhubarb Crumble

I'm rather partial to this recipe. The tangy-sweet mixture is so delightful, it's almost impossible to resist a second helping.

Serves 4

Tips

We still cook this "barbarian root" as rhubarb was once known with some reservations, but it adds a pleasing tartness to so many desserts. When combined with strawberry, it is superb.

If you're using frozen fruit, measure it frozen, then let thaw before cooking. If there is a lot of juice when it thaws, drain it off to prevent the dessert from being too saucy.

- • **Preheat oven to 400°F (200°C)**
- • **6-cup (1.5 L) shallow baking dish**

2 cups	chopped rhubarb (see Tips, left)	500 mL
2 cups	sliced strawberries	500 mL
1/4 cup	granulated sugar	60 mL
2 tbsp	all-purpose flour	30 mL

Crust

1 cup	all-purpose flour	250 mL
3/4 cup	packed brown sugar	175 mL
1/2 cup	melted butter	125 mL
1 tbsp	freshly squeezed lemon juice	15 mL
1/2 tsp	salt	2 mL

1. In a microwave-safe bowl, combine rhubarb, strawberries, granulated sugar and flour. Cover loosely and microwave on High for about 5 minutes, stirring twice, or until fruit is tender and liquid is slightly thickened. Transfer to baking dish.

2. *Crust:* In another bowl, combine flour, brown sugar, butter, lemon juice and salt until crumbly. Sprinkle over fruit mixture.

3. Bake in preheated oven for about 20 minutes or until fruit is bubbly and topping is crisp.

Pineapple Muffins

These pineapple muffins with pears will surprise you with every mouthful.

Makes 10 muffins

Tip

When mixing muffins, use a flexible silicone or rubber spatula and stir just until the dry ingredients are moistened. Overmixing will cause tough, rubbery muffins.

- **Preheat oven to 400°F (200°C)**
- **12-cup muffin pan, 10 cups lined with paper liners**

Topping

¼ cup	large-flake (old-fashioned) rolled oats	60 mL
¼ cup	packed brown sugar	60 mL
2 tbsp	chopped pecans	30 mL
2 tbsp	butter	30 mL
Pinch	ground cinnamon	Pinch
Pinch	ground ginger	Pinch

Muffins

1 cup	all-purpose flour	250 mL
¾ cup	large-flake (old-fashioned) rolled oats	175 mL
¼ cup	packed brown sugar	60 mL
2 tsp	baking powder	10 mL
½ tsp	baking soda	2 mL
¼ tsp	salt	1 mL
¼ tsp	ground nutmeg	1 mL
1	egg	1
⅓ cup	vegetable oil	75 mL
⅓ cup	plain yogurt	75 mL
1 tsp	grated lemon zest	5 mL
1 tbsp	freshly squeezed lemon juice	15 mL
1 cup	finely chopped fresh or drained canned pineapple	250 mL
½ cup	chopped fresh or drained canned pears	125 mL

1. *Topping:* In a bowl, combine oats, brown sugar, pecans, butter, cinnamon and ginger until crumbly. Set aside.

2. *Muffins:* In a large bowl, combine flour, oats, brown sugar, baking powder, baking soda, salt and nutmeg. In another bowl, whisk together egg, oil, yogurt, lemon zest and lemon juice. Stir in pineapple and pears. Pour over dry ingredients and stir just until moistened.

3. Spoon batter into prepared muffin cups and sprinkle with topping. Bake in preheated oven for about 15 minutes or until tops spring back when lightly touched. Let cool in pan on a wire rack for 5 minutes then transfer to the rack to cool completely.

Variation

Peach Hazelnut Muffins: Replace the pecans with hazelnuts and replace the pineapple and pears with $1\frac{1}{2}$ cups (375 mL) chopped fresh or drained canned peaches.

Blueberry Muffins

The moist texture of these muffins will charm you.

Makes 9 muffins

Tip
If using frozen blueberries, keep them frozen until just before you add them to the batter to reduce discoloration of the batter.

- **Preheat oven to 400°F (200°C)**
- **12-cup muffin pan, 9 cups greased or lined with paper liners**

1½ cups	all-purpose flour	375 mL
¼ cup	granulated sugar	60 mL
1 tbsp	baking powder	15 mL
½ tsp	baking soda	2 mL
½ tsp	salt	2 mL
2	eggs	2
¾ cup	vanilla-flavored yogurt	175 mL
½ cup	vanilla-flavored soy milk	125 mL
2 tbsp	vegetable oil	30 mL
¾ cup	fresh or frozen blueberries (see Tip, left)	175 mL

1. In a medium bowl, combine flour, sugar, baking powder, baking soda and salt. In another bowl, whisk together eggs, yogurt, soy milk and oil. Pour over dry ingredients and sprinkle with blueberries. Stir just until moistened.

2. Spoon batter into prepared muffin cups. Bake in preheated oven for about 20 minutes or until tops spring back when lightly touched. Let cool in pan on a wire rack for 5 minutes then transfer to the rack to cool completely.

Banana Muffins

This recipe allows you to rediscover the great taste of banana bread, but takes less time to make.

Makes 12 muffins

Tip

To toast nuts: In a small, dry skillet over medium heat, toast slivered almonds and chopped pecans, stirring constantly, for 3 to 4 minutes or until golden and fragrant. Immediately transfer to a bowl and let cool.

- **Preheat oven to 400°F (200°C)**
- **12-cup muffin pan, greased or lined with paper liners**

2 cups	all-purpose flour	500 mL
¼ cup	packed brown sugar	60 mL
1 tbsp	baking powder	15 mL
½ tsp	salt	2 mL
½ tsp	ground nutmeg	2 mL
½ cup	golden raisins	125 mL
¼ cup	toasted slivered almonds	60 mL
¼ cup	toasted chopped pecans	60 mL
1	egg	1
1 cup	mashed ripe bananas (about 3 small)	250 mL
½ cup	milk	125 mL
⅓ cup	vegetable oil	75 mL
1½ tsp	freshly squeezed lemon juice	7 mL

1. In a large bowl, combine flour, brown sugar, baking powder, salt, nutmeg, raisins, almonds and pecans. In another bowl, whisk together egg, bananas, milk, oil and lemon juice. Pour over dry ingredients and stir just until moistened.

2. Spoon batter into prepared muffin cups. Bake in preheated oven for about 20 minutes or until tops spring back when lightly touched. Let cool in pan on a wire rack for 5 minutes then transfer to the rack to cool completely.

Apple Muffins

This muffin recipe brings out all the subtle flavors of the apples.

Makes 8 large muffins

- • **Preheat oven to 350°F (180°C)**
- • **12-cup muffin pan, 8 cups greased or lined with paper liners**

Tips

Choose apples that keep their flavor when baked such as Granny Smith, Cortland, Empire, Golden Delicious or McIntosh.

You can also put a pecan half on each muffin before adding topping to decorate it.

Muffins

1½ cups	all-purpose flour	375 mL
½ tsp	baking soda	2 mL
½ tsp	ground cinnamon	2 mL
2	eggs	2
½ cup	packed brown sugar	125 mL
½ cup	vegetable oil	125 mL
1 tsp	vanilla extract	5 mL
2 cups	chopped apples (see Tips, left)	500 mL
½ cup	toasted chopped pecans	125 mL

Topping

1 tsp	granulated sugar	5 mL
¼ tsp	ground cinnamon	1 mL

1. *Muffins:* In a large bowl, combine flour, baking soda and cinnamon. In another bowl, whisk together eggs, brown sugar, oil and vanilla. Pour over dry ingredients and sprinkle with apples and pecans. Stir just until moistened. Spoon batter into prepared muffin cups.

2. *Topping:* In a small bowl, combine sugar and cinnamon. Sprinkle on top of muffins.

3. Bake in preheated oven for 15 to 20 minutes or until tops spring back when lightly touched. Let cool in pan on a wire rack for 5 minutes then transfer to the rack to cool completely.

Oatmeal Cookies

Here is the recipe that I invented the night before I went into labor with my first child. Maternity is inspiring!

Makes about 30 cookies

Tips

If you are baking more than one sheet of cookies at a time, position the oven racks in the upper and lower thirds of the oven and place one sheet on each rack. Switch the sheets on the racks partway through baking time to ensure even baking.

Soft cookies such as these ones are best stored in an airtight container at room temperature for up to 3 days. For longer storage, layer between parchment paper and freeze for up to 3 months.

- **Preheat oven to 400°F (200°C)**
- **Baking sheets, lined with parchment paper or greased**

1 cup	whole wheat flour	250 mL
1 cup	large-flake (old-fashioned) rolled oats	250 mL
½ cup	packed brown sugar	125 mL
½ cup	raisins	125 mL
⅓ cup	sunflower seeds	75 mL
⅓ cup	chopped walnuts	75 mL
1 tsp	baking powder	5 mL
½ tsp	baking soda	2 mL
½ tsp	salt	2 mL
¼ tsp	ground cinnamon	1 mL
1	egg, beaten	1
½ cup	unsweetened applesauce	125 mL
1 tbsp	vegetable oil	15 mL
1 tsp	vanilla extract	5 mL

1. In a large bowl, combine flour, oats, brown sugar, raisins, sunflower seeds, walnuts, baking powder, baking soda, salt, cinnamon, egg, applesauce, oil and vanilla.

2. Drop heaping tablespoonfuls (15 mL) of dough at least 2 inches (5 cm) apart on prepared baking sheets.

3. Bake in preheated oven for about 15 minutes or until edges are set and tops spring back when lightly touched. Let cool on pans on a wire rack for 5 minutes then transfer to the rack to cool completely.

Chocolate Chip Cookies

Who can pass up a batch of chocolate chip cookies? No one!

Makes 20 cookies

Tips

If you are baking more than one sheet of cookies at a time, position the oven racks in the upper and lower thirds of the oven and place one sheet on each rack. Switch the sheets on the racks partway through baking time to ensure even baking.

Crisp cookies, such as these, are best stored in a cookie tin at room temperature for up to 5 days. For longer storage, layer between parchment paper in an airtight container and freeze for up to 3 months.

- Preheat oven to 400°F (200°C)
- Baking sheets, lined with parchment paper or greased

1 cup	all-purpose flour	250 mL
¾ cup	chocolate chips	175 mL
½ cup	chopped walnuts	125 mL
½ cup	packed brown sugar	125 mL
½ tsp	baking powder	2 mL
½ tsp	salt	2 mL
1	egg, beaten	1
⅓ cup	melted butter	75 mL
½ tsp	vanilla extract	2 mL

1. In a bowl, combine flour, chocolate chips, walnuts, brown sugar, baking powder, salt, egg, butter and vanilla.

2. Drop dough by heaping tablespoonfuls (15 mL) at least 2 inches (5 cm) apart onto prepared baking sheets. Use a fork to flatten them. Bake in preheated oven for about 10 minutes or until golden around the edges and set in the center. Let cool on pans on a wire rack for 5 minutes then transfer to the rack to cool completely.

Peanut Butter Cookies

You can halve this recipe if you don't live with an army of hungry little ones. But, if you do make more than you can eat at once, these cookies can also be frozen (see Tips, below).

Makes about 40 cookies

Tips

If you are baking more than one sheet of cookies at a time, position the oven racks in the upper and lower thirds of the oven and place one sheet on each rack. Switch the sheets on the racks partway through baking time to ensure even baking.

Crisp cookies, such as these, are best stored in a cookie tin at room temperature for up to 5 days. For longer storage, layer between parchment paper in an airtight container and freeze for up to 3 months.

- **Preheat oven to 400°F (200°C)**
- **Baking sheets, lined with parchment paper or greased**

2 cups	all-purpose flour	500 mL
1 cup	packed brown sugar	250 mL
1/2 cup	granulated sugar	125 mL
2 tsp	baking powder	10 mL
2	eggs, beaten	2
1 cup	crunchy peanut butter	250 mL
1/2 cup	melted butter	125 mL
1/4 cup	peanuts	60 mL
1/4 cup	chocolate chips, optional	60 mL

1. In a bowl, combine flour, brown sugar, granulated sugar, baking powder, eggs, peanut butter and melted butter.

2. Scoop heaping tablespoonfuls (15 mL) of dough and roll each into a ball. Place at least 2 inches (5 cm) apart on prepared baking sheets. Use a fork to flatten them. Press a few peanuts and chocolate chips, if using, on each cookie to decorate it.

3. Bake in preheated oven for about 15 minutes or until golden brown around the edges and set in the center. Let cool on pans on a wire rack for 5 minutes then transfer to the rack to cool completely.

Granola Bars

These are the perfect snack to answer a little hunger pang in the afternoon.

Makes about 20 bars

Tip

Store granola bars in an airtight container at room temperature for up to 3 days or layer between waxed or parchment paper and freeze for up to 3 months.

- Preheat oven to 400°F (200°C)
- 8-inch (20 cm) square metal baking pan, lined with parchment paper

1	egg	1
¼ cup	packed brown sugar	60 mL
¼ cup	vegetable oil	60 mL
1½ cups	large-flake (old-fashioned) rolled oats	375 mL
½ cup	all-purpose flour	125 mL
½ cup	sweetened shredded coconut	125 mL
¼ cup	raisins	60 mL
¼ cup	green pumpkin seeds (pepitas)	60 mL
¼ tsp	salt	1 mL
¼ tsp	baking soda	1 mL

1. In a bowl, whisk together egg, brown sugar and oil. Stir in oats, flour, coconut, raisins, pumpkin seeds, salt and baking soda.

2. Press into bottom of prepared pan (it will be fairly thin). Bake in preheated oven for about 15 minutes or until golden and set. Let cool completely in pan on a wire rack. Transfer to a cutting board, peel off parchment paper and cut into bars.

Date Mini-Bites

In these sweet treats, dates are a marvelous replacement for much of the sugar.

Makes 24 mini-bites

Tips

If you are baking more than one sheet of cookies at a time, position the oven racks in the upper and lower thirds of the oven and place one sheet on each rack. Switch the sheets on the racks partway through baking time to ensure even baking.

Soft cookies such as these ones are best stored in an airtight container at room temperature for up to 3 days. For longer storage, layer between parchment paper and freeze for up to 3 months.

- **Preheat oven to 400°F (200°C)**
- **Baking sheet, lined with parchment paper**

1 cup	finely chopped dates	250 mL
¾ cup	large-flake (old-fashioned) rolled oats	175 mL
½ cup	all-purpose flour	125 mL
¼ cup	sunflower seeds	60 mL
2 tbsp	packed brown sugar	30 mL
½ tsp	baking soda	2 mL
¼ tsp	ground cinnamon	1 mL
¼ tsp	salt	1 mL
1	egg, beaten	1
¼ cup	melted butter	60 mL
¼ cup	plain yogurt	60 mL
1 tsp	vanilla extract	5 mL

1. In a large bowl, combine dates, oats, flour, sunflower seeds, brown sugar, baking soda, cinnamon, salt, egg, butter, yogurt and vanilla.

2. Drop dough by heaping tablespoonfuls (15 mL) at least 2 inches (5 cm) apart onto prepared baking sheets.

3. Bake in preheated oven for about 15 minutes or until tops spring back when lightly touched. Let cool on pans on a wire rack for 5 minutes then transfer to the rack to cool completely.

Date Squares

All the great flavor and sweetness of dates are found in the middle of a perfect square — success guaranteed!

Makes 16 squares

- Preheat oven to 400°F (200°C)
- 8-inch (20 cm) square metal baking pan, lined with parchment paper

Tips

To cook the date filling on the stovetop instead of the microwave, combine ingredients in a saucepan and bring to a simmer over medium-high heat. Reduce heat and boil gently, stirring often, for about 10 minutes or until dates are soft and mixture is thickened.

Store date squares in an airtight container, layered with parchment paper or waxed paper, at room temperature for up to 2 days. For longer storage, freeze for up to 3 months.

Date Filling

2 cups	chopped dates	500 mL
1/3 cup	packed brown sugar	75 mL
1 tbsp	all-purpose flour	15 mL
1 1/4 cups	water	300 mL
1 tsp	vanilla extract	5 mL

Crust

2 cups	quick-cooking rolled oats	500 mL
1 cup	all-purpose flour	250 mL
1/2 cup	packed brown sugar	125 mL
1 tsp	baking soda	5 mL
3/4 cup	melted butter	175 mL

1. *Date Filling:* In a microwave–safe bowl, combine dates, brown sugar, flour and water. Microwave on High for about 5 minutes or until dates are softened and mixture is thickened. Let cool completely. Stir in vanilla.

2. *Crust:* Meanwhile, in a bowl, combine oats, flour, brown sugar, baking soda and melted butter. Press half the oatmeal mixture into prepared baking pan. Spread date filling on top, then cover with the rest of the oatmeal mixture, pressing down lightly.

3. Bake in preheated oven for about 20 minutes or until crumbs are golden brown. Let cool completely in pan on a wire rack. Cut into squares.

Grandmother's Sugar Pie

It's easy to understand why this recipe has been passed down from generation to generation. It's easy, light and divinely delicious.

Serves 6

Tip

A traditional French-Canadian favorite baked by Grandma and Great Grandma, this pie combines common pantry ingredients in an uncommonly good creation.

- **Preheat oven to 350°F (180°)**

1	unbaked 9-inch (23 cm) pie crust	1
⅔ cup	packed brown sugar	150 mL
1 tbsp	cornstarch	15 mL
⅔ cup	heavy or whipping (35%) cream	150 mL
	Pecans or walnut halves, optional	

1. In a bowl, whisk together brown sugar, cornstarch and cream. Pour into pie crust.

2. Top with pecans or walnuts, if using.

3. Bake in preheated oven for 25 to 30 minutes or until edges are puffed and center is just set. Let cool completely in pie plate on a wire rack.

Lemon Pie

Four steps and three layers add up to a totally delectable dessert. Don't forget to leave some for the people you love!

Serves 6

Tip
You can reserve a few crumbs from the crust to sprinkle on top of the pie at the very end.

- **Preheat oven to 375°F (190°C)**
- **9-inch (23 cm) pie plate**

Shell

1¼ cups	graham cracker crumbs	300 mL
1 tbsp	granulated sugar	15 mL
¼ cup	butter	60 mL

Filling

1 cup	granulated sugar	250 mL
¼ cup	cornstarch	60 mL
¼ tsp	salt	1 mL
3	egg yolks (see Tips, right)	3
1½ cups	water	375 mL
	Grated zest of half a lemon	
¼ cup	freshly squeezed lemon juice	60 mL
1 tbsp	butter	15 mL

Meringue

3	egg whites, at room temperature	3
3 tbsp	granulated sugar	45 mL

1. *Shell:* In a microwave-safe bowl, combine graham cracker crumbs, sugar and butter. Microwave on Medium-Low (30%) for about 2 minutes or until butter is melted. Stir to combine and press into pie plate.

2. *Filling:* In a saucepan, whisk together sugar, cornstarch, salt, egg yolks, water, lemon zest, lemon juice and butter. Cook over medium heat, whisking constantly, for about 8 minutes or until thickened. Spoon into pie shell.

3. *Meringue:* In a bowl, using an electric mixer, beat egg whites until soft peaks form. Gradually beat in sugar. Beat until stiff, glossy peaks form. Spoon meringue on top of the filling, spreading to cover filling entirely and making sure meringue touches the crust.

4. Bake in preheated oven for about 10 minutes or until meringue is golden. Let cool completely in pie plate on a wire rack.

Ricotta Coconut Cake

A cake so quick to mix, it makes up for the 40 minutes of baking time.

Serves 4 to 6

Tip
Ricotta is a fresh cheese that is part of Italian culinary history. It is used mainly in pasta dishes and desserts.

- **Preheat oven to 400°F (200°C)**
- **9-inch (23 cm) springform pan, greased and bottom lined with parchment paper**

2 cups	ricotta cheese (see Tip, left)	500 mL
3	eggs, beaten	3
⅓ cup	granulated sugar	75 mL
⅓ cup	golden raisins	75 mL
⅓ cup	unsweetened shredded coconut	75 mL
2 tbsp	all-purpose flour	30 mL
	Grated zest of half a lemon	
1 tbsp	freshly squeezed lemon juice	15 mL
1 tsp	vanilla extract	5 mL

1. In a bowl, combine ricotta cheese, eggs, sugar, raisins, coconut, flour, lemon zest, lemon juice and vanilla. Spread into prepared pan.

2. Bake in preheated oven for about 40 minutes or until a tester inserted in the center comes out clean. Let cool completely in pan on a wire rack. Run a knife around edge and remove ring to serve.

Creamy Fruit Delight

My son purrs at the thought of this dish. It's a great dessert but also have it for breakfast or to satisfy a little hunger pang in the afternoon.

Serves 4

Tip

When purchasing sunflower seeds and flax seeds, be sure they're fresh with no strong, rancid aroma. Store both in an airtight container in the freezer for optimal freshness. You can toast them lightly in a dry skillet over medium heat, stirring constantly, for 1 to 2 minutes to enhance the flavor before using. Immediately transfer to a bowl and let cool before grinding.

½ cup	large-flake (old-fashioned) rolled oats	125 mL
½ cup	sunflower seeds	125 mL
½ cup	flax seeds	125 mL
½ cup	plain yogurt	125 mL
½ cup	freshly squeezed grapefruit juice	125 mL
¼ cup	freshly squeezed lemon juice	60 mL
1	banana, mashed	1

1. In a clean coffee grinder or a mini chopper, grind oats, sunflower seeds and flax seeds until fine crumbs. Transfer to a bowl.

2. Add yogurt, grapefruit juice, lemon juice and banana and stir to combine. Serve immediately.

Library and Archives Canada Cataloguing in Publication

Morin, Marie-Claude
    The best 30-minute vegetarian recipes / Marie-Claude Morin.

Includes index.
ISBN 978-0-7788-0266-2

1.Vegetarian cooking. 2. Quick and easy cooking.
I.Title. II.Title: Best thirty-minute vegetarian recipes.

TX837.M676 2011   641.5'636   C2010-907398-3

Index

v = variation

A

Alfalfa sprouts
  Grilled Vegetable
    Sandwiches, 88
  Mandoline Salad, 79
All-Dressed Pizza, 101
Almonds
  Banana Muffins, 169
  Basmati Rice with Peas
    and Nuts, 154
  Chicory Salad, 80
  Curry Couscous, 124
  toasting, 134
  Wild Rice Salad, 65
Appetizers
  Baked Camembert, 28
  Bean Dip, 31
  Brie Baguette Bites, 24
  Bruschetta Baguette Bites,
    26
  Cherry Tomatoes with
    Cheese, 18
  Cherry Tomatoes with
    Zesty Cheese (v), 18
  Chili Black Bean Dip (v),
    33
  Cilantro Avocado Salsa (v),
    21
  Cilantro Salsa, 21
  Curry Dip, 32
  Fava Bean Dip, 33
  Feta Cheese Bites, 37
  Fresh Herb Hummus (v),
    22
  Goat Cheese Bites, 36
  Guacamole, 20
  Hummus, 22
  Mini Pitas with Eggs, 39
  Mushroom Bites, 35
  Onion Baguette Bites, 27
  Orange Pepper Dip, 34
  Parmesan Baguette Bites,
    25
  Polenta Cakes, 29
  Quesadillas, 19
  Sun-Dried Tomato Baked
    Camembert (v), 28
  Thai Red Curry Dip (v),
    32

Toasted Pita Chips, 23
Tofu Cakes, 30
Vegetable Roll-Ups, 38
Apple cider vinegar, 71
Apples, 162, 163
  Apple Cherry Crisp (v),
    163
  Apple Cranberry Crisp (v),
    163
  Apple Crisp, 163
  Apple Delight, 162
  Apple Muffins, 170
Applesauce
  Oatmeal Cookies, 171
Artichokes, 141
  Lemony Artichokes, 141
Arugula, 64
  Divine Salad, 68
  Hint of Orange Salad, 64
Asiago cheese
  Zesty Four-Cheese Pizza
    (v), 102
Asian Mandoline Salad (v),
  79
Asian Salad, 62
Asparagus, 140
  Asparagus in Vinaigrette,
    140
  Avocado Salad, 70
  Polenta Mountain, 132
  Rice Quiche, 90
  Vegetable Roll-Ups, 38
Avocados
  Avocado Salad, 70
  Cilantro Avocado Salsa (v),
    21
  Guacamole, 20
  Hint of Orange Salad, 64

B

Bagel Melt, 94
Baguettes
  Bread Salad, 77
  Cheese Fondue, 130
  Brie Baguette Bites, 24
  Bruschetta Baguette Bites,
    26
  Onion Baguette Bites, 27
  Onion Soup, 45
  Parmesan Baguette Bites,
    25

Roasted Red Pepper
    Bread Salad (v), 77
  Sunny-Side Up Western
    Sandwiches, 89
Baked Camembert, 28
Balsamic vinegar, 65
Banana
  Banana Honey Fritters,
    158
  Banana Muffins, 169
  Creamy Fruit Delight,
    181
Basil
  Bread Salad, 77
  Parmesan Baguette Bites
    (v), 25
  Pasta Salad with Basil
    Pesto, 73
Basil Pesto, 73
  Baked Camembert, 28
  Pasta Salad with Basil
    Pesto, 73
  Pasta with Goat Cheese,
    117
  Pesto Pizza, 103
Basmati rice, 91
Basmati Rice with Peas and
  Nuts, 154
Bean Dip, 31
Bean sprouts, 134
  Asian Salad, 62
  Crispy Salad, 69
  Tofu Soup, 55
  Vegetable Stir-Fry, 127
  Vegetarian Chop Suey,
    134
  Warm Potato Salad, 75
Beans, 12. See also individual
  varieties
  Legume Salad, 58
  Three-Bean Soup, 47
Beans, black
  Burritos, 104
  Chili Black Bean Dip (v),
    33
  Three-Bean Omelet, 96
Beans, fava
  Fava Bean Dip, 33
  Rice Soup, 42
Beans, green. See Green
  beans

Beans, kidney
  Bean Dip, 31
  Chili sin Carne, 111
  Hearty Minestrone, 84
  Three-Bean Omelet, 96
Beans, navy
  Bean Dip, 31
Beans, white
  Vegetable Paella, 135
Béchamel
  Spinach Ricotta
    Cannelloni, 122
Bell pepper, 34
  All-Dressed Pizza, 101
  Burritos, 104
  Couscous Salad, 66
  Couscous with Prunes,
    120
  Frittata, 100
  Gazpacho, 53
  Goat Cheese Bites, 36
  Green Mango Salad (v),
    76
  Legume Salad, 58
  Lentils with Cumin, 109
  Orange Pepper Dip, 34
  Rice with Cranberries and
    Curry, 155
  Roasted Red Pepper
    Bread Salad (v), 77
  Spinach, Roasted Pepper
    and Basil Cannelloni (v),
    123
  Stuffed Peppers, 137
  Three-Bean Omelet, 96
  Tofu Brochettes, 126
  Vegetable Curry, 128
  Vegetable Roll-Ups, 38
  Zucchini Roasted Red
    Pepper Mini Lasagnas
    (v), 107
Blueberries
  Blueberry Muffins, 168
  Fruit Parfait, 160
Blue cheese
  Blue Cheese Salad, 81
  Blue Pasta, 115
  Brie Baguette Bites (v),
    24
  Zesty Four-Cheese Pizza
    (v), 102
Bread Salad, 77
Brie cheese
  Brie Baguette Bites, 24
  Mini Lasagnas, 106

Broccoli
  Broccoli and Cheddar
    Soup, 51
  Broccoli in Creamy Sauce,
    145
  Rice Quiche, 90
  Spinach Quiche, 92
  Vegetable Curry, 128
  Vegetable Stir-Fry, 127
Brochettes
  Tofu Brochettes, 126
Bruschetta Baguette Bites, 26
Brussels sprouts
  Pasta and Brussels Sprouts
    Salad, 72
Bulgur, 67
  Ratatouille with Bulgur
    (v), 121
  Tabbouleh, 67
Burgers
  Veggie Burger, 129
Burritos, 104

C

Cabbage
  Asian Mandoline Salad (v),
    79
  Asian Salad (v), 62
  Hearty Minestrone, 84
  Mandoline Salad, 79
Cakes. See Desserts
Camembert
  Baked Camembert, 28
Capers
  Lentil Pie, 86
Carrots
  All-Dressed Pizza, 101
  Carrot and Turnip Soup,
    50
  Chickpea Stew, 105
  Corn Soup, 49
  Couscous with Prunes,
    120
  Fragrant Carrots, 143
  Hearty Minestrone, 84
  Julienne Vegetable Soup, 52
  Lentil Ratatouille, 110
  Lentil Soup, 48
  Lentils with Cumin, 109
  Mandoline Salad, 79
  Pasta and Brussels Sprouts
    Salad, 72
  Polenta Mountain, 132
  Russian Salad, 74
  Spaghetti Sauce, 112

Stuffed Zucchini, 150
Tofu Tacos, 113
Vegetable Curry, 128
Vegetable Stir-Fry, 127
Warm Potato Salad, 75
Cauliflower
  Broccoli and Cheddar
    Soup (v), 51
  Cauliflower Omelet, 95
  Cauliflower with Curry,
    144
  Warm Potato Salad, 75
Cheddar cheese, 27, 119
  All-Dressed Pizza, 101
  Broccoli and Cheddar
    Soup, 51
  Bruschetta Baguette Bites,
    26
  Club Sandwich, 97
  Four-Cheese Pizza, 102
  Lentil Pie, 86
  Macaroni with Tomato and
    Cheese, 118
  Onion Baguette Bites, 27
  Pecan Paradise Pasta, 119
  Pesto Pizza, 103
  Quesadillas, 19
  Rice Quiche, 90
  Stuffed Squash, 136
  Stuffed Zucchini, 150
Cheese, 12. See also
    individual varieties
  Bagel Melt, 94
  Cheese Fondue, 130
  Cherry Tomatoes with
    Zesty Cheese (v), 18
  Sunny-Side Up Western
    Sandwiches, 89
Cherries
  Apple Cherry Crisp (v),
    163
  Fruit with Cream, 159
Cherry Tomatoes with
    Cheese, 18
Cherry Tomatoes with Zesty
    Cheese (v), 18
Chestnuts
  Tofu Soup, 55
  Vegetable Curry, 128
  Vegetable Stir-Fry, 127
Chickpeas
  Chickpea Salad (v), 59
  Chickpea Stew, 105
  Couscous with Prunes,
    120

Fresh Herb Hummus (v), 22
Hummus, 22
Stuffed Zucchini, 150
Three-Bean Omelet, 96
Chicory Salad, 80
Chili Black Bean Dip (v), 33
Chili sauce
    Curry Dip, 32
Chili sin Carne, 111
Chocolate chips
    Chocolate Chip Cookies, 172
    Peanut Butter Cookies, 173
Chop Suey, Vegetarian, 134
Cilantro, 76
    Cilantro Avocado Salsa (v), 21
    Cilantro Salsa, 21
Club Sandwich, 97
Coconut milk
    Hard-Boiled Eggs with Lentils, 99
    Pea Soup, 54
    Tofu with Peanut Sauce, 125
    Vegetable Curry, 128
Coconuts
    Granola Bars, 174
    Ricotta Coconut Cake, 180
Cookies
    Chocolate Chip Cookies, 172
    Oatmeal Cookies, 171
    Peanut Butter Cookies, 173
Corn
    Chili sin Carne, 111
    Corn Soup, 49
    Curry Couscous, 124
    Russian Salad, 74
    Sweet Potato Shepherd's Pie, 131
Cornmeal
    Polenta Cakes, 29
    Polenta Mountain, 132
    Polenta Mountain Arrabbiata (v), 133
Cottage cheese
    Broccoli in Creamy Sauce, 145
    Orange Pepper Dip, 34

Couscous, 13
    Couscous Salad, 66
    Couscous with Prunes, 120
    Curry Couscous, 124
Cranberries, dried, 155
    Apple Cranberry Crisp (v), 163
    Feta Cheese Bites, 37
    Rice with Cranberries and Curry, 155
Cream cheese
    Cherry Tomatoes with Cheese, 18
    Parmesan Baguette Bites, 25
    Red Pasta, 116
Creamy Fruit Delight, 181
Creamy Lentils, 108
Crisps
    Apple Cherry Crisp (v), 163
    Apple Cranberry Crisp (v), 163
    Apple Crisp, 163
Crispy Salad, 69
Crumble
    Strawberry Rhubarb Crumble, 165
Cucumber
    Bread Salad, 77
    Couscous Salad, 66
    Divine Salad, 68
    Greek Salad, 61
    Hint of Orange Salad, 64
    Mandoline Salad, 79
    Tofu Pita Sandwiches, 93
Curry Couscous, 124
Curry Dip, 32

D
Date Mini-Bites, 175
Date Squares, 176
Desserts
    Apple Cherry Crisp (v), 163
    Apple Cranberry Crisp (v), 163
    Apple Crisp, 163
    Apple Delight, 162
    Apple Muffins, 170
    Banana Honey Fritters, 158
    Banana Muffins, 169
    Blueberry Muffins, 168

Chocolate Chip Cookies, 172
Creamy Fruit Delight, 181
Date Mini-Bites, 175
Date Squares, 176
Fruit Parfait, 160
Fruit with Cream, 159
Grandmother's Sugar Pie, 177
Granola Bars, 174
Honey Ginger Three-Fruit Salad (v), 161
Lemon Pie, 178
Oatmeal Cookies, 171
Peach Hazelnut Muffins (v), 167
Peach Melba Parfait (v), 160
Peanut Butter Cookies, 173
Pineapple Muffins, 166
Ricotta Coconut Cake, 180
Strawberry Mounds, 164
Three-Fruit Salad, 161
Dips
    Bean Dip, 31
    Chili Black Bean Dip (v), 33
    Cilantro Salsa, 21
    Curry Dip, 32
    Fava Bean Dip, 33
    Fresh Herb Hummus (v), 22
    Guacamole, 20
    Hummus, 22
    Orange Pepper Dip, 34
    Thai Red Curry Dip (v), 32
Divine Salad, 68
Double-Tomato Pesto Pizza (v), 103

E
Eggplant
    Eggplant with Tomato, 151
    Lentil Ratatouille, 110
    Ratatouille with Bulgur (v), 121
Eggs, 179
    Cauliflower Omelet, 95
    Frittata, 100
    Spinach Quiche, 92
    Stuffed Tomato with Egg, 98

Eggs (continued)
  Sunny-Side Up Western
    Sandwiches, 89
  Three-Bean Omelet, 96
Eggs, hard-boiled, 60
  Chicory Salad, 80
  Hard-Boiled Eggs with
    Lentils, 99
  Mini Pitas with Eggs, 39
  Russian Salad, 74
  Spanish Salad, 60
Emmental cheese
  Spinach Ricotta
    Cannelloni, 122
Endives
  Hint of Orange Salad, 64

F

Fava Bean Dip, 33
Feta cheese, 37
  Chickpea Salad (v), 59
  Curry Dip, 32
  Divine Salad, 68
  Feta Cheese Bites, 37
  Greek Salad, 61
  Orange Pepper Dip, 34
  Spaghetti Squash Salad,
    78
  Thai Red Curry Dip (v),
    32
Fondue
  Cheese Fondue, 130
Four-Cheese Pizza, 102
Fragrant Carrots, 143
Fresh Herb Hummus (v), 22
Frisée, 80
  Chicory Salad, 80
Frittata, 100
Fruits. See also individual
    varieties
  Creamy Fruit Delight, 181
  Fruit Parfait, 160
  Fruit with Cream, 159
  Honey Ginger Three-Fruit
    Salad (v), 161
  Peach Melba Parfait (v),
    160
  Three-Fruit Salad, 161
Fusilli. See also Pasta
  Green Pasta, 114

G

Garam masala, 108
  Creamy Lentils, 108
Gazpacho, 53

Goat cheese
  Club Sandwich, 97
  Creamy Lentils, 108
  Four-Cheese Pizza, 102
  Goat Cheese Bites, 36
  Grilled Vegetable
    Sandwiches, 88
  Pasta with Goat Cheese,
    117
  Quesadillas, 19
  Stuffed Peppers, 137
  Tofu Cakes, 30
Gorgonzola cheese, Blue
    Cheese Salad, 81
Grandmother's Sugar Pie, 177
Granola Bars, 174
Grapefruit juice, Creamy
    Fruit Delight, 181
Grapefruit, Avocado Salad, 70
Grapes, Fruit with Cream,
    159
Greek Salad, 61
Green beans
  Rice Quiche (v), 90
  Beans with Tomatoes, 142
  Green Pasta, 114
  Hearts of Palm Salad, 71
  Legume Salad, 58
  Vegetable Paella, 135
  Vegetable Paella, 135
Green Mango Salad (v), 76
Green Pasta, 114
Green peas
  Basmati Rice with Peas
    and Nuts, 154
  Crispy Salad, 69
  Curry Couscous, 124
  Green Pasta, 114
  Pea Soup, 54
  Risotto with Sun-Dried
    Tomatoes, 85
  Russian Salad, 74
Grilled Vegetable
    Sandwiches, 88
Gruyère cheese
  Onion Soup, 45
  Swiss Chard Gratin, 148
Guacamole, 20

H

Hard-Boiled Eggs with
    Lentils, 99
Havarti cheese
  All-Dressed Pizza, 101
  Four-Cheese Pizza, 102

Hazelnuts
  Brie Baguette Bites (v), 24
  Peach Hazelnut Muffins
    (v), 167
Hearts of Palm Salad, 71
Hearty Minestrone, 84
Herbes de Provence, 47
Hint of Orange Salad, 64
Honey Ginger Three-Fruit
    Salad (v), 161
Hummus, 22
  Fresh Herb Hummus (v),
    22
  Vegetable Roll-Ups, 38

J

Julienne, 93
Julienne Vegetable Soup, 52

K

Kale
  Swiss Chard Gratin (v),
    148

L

Lasagna. See also Pasta
  Mini Lasagnas, 106
  Zucchini Roasted Red
    Pepper Mini Lasagnas
    (v), 107
Leek and Potato Soup, 43
Legumes, 12
Legume Salad, 58
Lemon juice
  Creamy Fruit Delight, 181
  Hummus, 22
  Lemon Pie, 178
  Lemony Artichokes, 141
  Mandoline Salad, 79
  Ricotta Coconut Cake,
    180
Lentils, 48
  Creamy Lentils, 108
  Hard-Boiled Eggs with
    Lentils, 99
  Lentil Pie, 86
  Lentil Ratatouille, 110
  Lentil Salad, 59
  Lentil Soup, 48
  Lentils with Cumin, 109
  Stuffed Peppers, 137
Lettuce
  Club Sandwich, 97
  Divine Salad, 68
  Spanish Salad, 60

Linguini. *See also* Pasta
  Blue Pasta, 115

M

Macaroni. *See also* Pasta
  Macaroni with Tomato and
    Cheese, 118
  Three-Bean Soup, 47
Mandoline Salad, 79
Mangos
  Green Mango Salad (v), 76
  Mango Salad, 76
Mayonnaise
  Curry Dip, 32
  Fava Bean Dip, 33
  Mini Pitas with Eggs, 39
  Patatas Bravas, 146
  Russian Salad, 74
Measuring ingredients, 15
Melons
  Fruit with Cream, 159
  Three-Fruit Salad, 161
Meringues, 179
Mini Lasagnas, 106
Mini Pitas with Eggs, 39
Mozzarella cheese
  Chickpea Salad (v), 59
  Double-Tomato Pesto
    Pizza (v), 103
  Eggplant with Tomato, 151
  Zucchini Roasted Red
    Pepper Mini Lasagnas
    (v), 107
Muffins
  Apple Muffins, 170
  Banana Muffins, 169
  Blueberry Muffins, 168
  Peach Hazelnut Muffins
    (v), 167
  Pineapple Muffins, 166
  Sweet Potato Muffins, 147
Mushrooms
  Bagel Melt, 94
  Burritos, 104
  Grilled Vegetable
    Sandwiches, 88
  Julienne Vegetable Soup, 52
  Mini Lasagnas, 106
  Mushroom Bites, 35
  Mushroom Soup, 46
  Rice Quiche, 90
  Spaghetti Squash Salad, 78
  Stuffed Squash, 136
  Tofu Brochettes, 126
  Tofu Tacos, 113

Vegetable Curry, 128
Vegetable Stir-Fry, 127
Vegetarian Chop Suey, 134

N

Nuts, 13, 28. *See also*
    individual varieties
  Basmati Rice with Peas
    and Nuts, 154
  Divine Salad, 68
  toasting, 169

O

Oats
  Apple Crisp, 163
  Creamy Fruit Delight, 181
  Date Mini-Bites, 175
  Date Squares, 176
  Granola Bars, 174
  Oatmeal Cookies, 171
  Pineapple Muffins, 166
  Veggie Burger, 129
Oil, 13
Olives
  Chicory Salad, 80
  Divine Salad, 68
  Greek Salad, 61
  Hearts of Palm Salad, 71
  Hint of Orange Salad, 64
  kalamata, 61
  Mini Pitas with Eggs, 39
  Polenta Mountain, 132
  Russian Salad, 74
  Spaghetti Squash Salad, 78
  Spanish Salad, 60
  Tofu Cakes, 30
Omelets
  Cauliflower Omelet, 95
  Frittata, 100
  Three-Bean Omelet, 96
Onion Baguette Bites, 27
Onion Pie, 87
Onion Soup, 45
Onions, caramelizing, 118
Orange Pepper Dip, 34
Oven-Roasted Vegetables,
  152

P

Paella, 15
  Vegetable, 135
Parmesan cheese
  Broccoli in Creamy Sauce,
    145
  Chicory Salad, 80

Crispy Salad, 69
Divine Salad, 68
Four-Cheese Pizza, 102
Hearty Minestrone, 84
Parmesan Baguette Bites,
  25
Pasta Salad with Basil
  Pesto, 73
Risotto with Sun-Dried
  Tomatoes, 85
Russian Salad, 74
Spinach Quiche, 92
Tofu Cakes (v), 30
Vegetarian Chop Suey,
  134
Parsnips
  Oven-Roasted Vegetables,
    152
Pasta, 116
  Blue Pasta, 115
  Frittata, 100
  Green Pasta, 114
  Julienne Vegetable Soup,
    52
  Macaroni with Tomato and
    Cheese, 118
  Mini Lasagnas, 106
  Pasta and Brussels Sprouts
    Salad, 72
  Pasta Salad with Basil
    Pesto, 73
  Pasta with Goat Cheese,
    117
  Pecan Paradise Pasta, 119
  Red Pasta, 116
  Spinach Ricotta
    Cannelloni, 122
  Spinach, Roasted Pepper
    and Basil Cannelloni (v),
    123
  Three-Bean Soup, 47
  Tofu Soup, 55
  Zucchini Roasted Red
    Pepper Mini Lasagnas
    (v), 107
Patatas Bravas, 146
Pea Soup, 54
Peach Hazelnut Muffins (v),
  167
Peach Melba Parfait (v), 160
Peanut butter
  Peanut Butter Cookies,
    173
  Tofu with Peanut Sauce,
    125

Peanuts
    Peanut Butter Cookies,
      173
    Vegetable Stir-Fry, 127
Pears
    Blue Cheese Salad, 81
    Pineapple Muffins, 166
Peas. *See* Green peas
Pecans
    Apple Muffins, 170
    Baked Camembert, 28
    Banana Muffins, 169
    Blue Cheese Salad, 81
    Brie Baguette Bites, 24
    Grandmother's Sugar Pie,
      177
    Pecan Paradise Pasta, 119
    Pineapple Muffins, 166
Penne
    Pasta Salad with Basil
      Pesto, 73
Pesto, 73, 103
Pesto Pizza, 103
Pickles
    Chicory Salad, 80
    Mini Pitas with Eggs, 39
    Tofu Pita Sandwiches, 93
Pies, savory
    Lentil Pie, 86
    Onion Pie, 87
    Spinach Quiche, 92
Pies, sweet
    Lemon Pie, 178
Pineapple
    Fruit Parfait, 160
    Pineapple Muffins, 166
    Three-Fruit Salad, 161
Pine nuts, 62
    Asian Salad, 62
    Blue Pasta, 115
    Cherry Tomatoes with
      Cheese, 18
    Pasta Salad with Basil
      Pesto, 73
    Risotto with Sun-Dried
      Tomatoes, 85
    Spinach Quiche, 92
    Sun-Dried Tomato Baked
      Camembert (v), 28
    toasting, 85
    Wild Rice Salad, 65
Pita bread
    All-Dressed Pizza, 101
    Four-Cheese Pizza, 102
    Mini Pitas with Eggs, 39

    Toasted Pita Chips, 23
    Tofu Pita Sandwiches, 93
Pizzas
    All-Dressed Pizza, 101
    Double-Tomato Pesto
      Pizza (v), 103
    Four-Cheese Pizza, 102
    Pesto Pizza, 103
    Zesty Four-Cheese Pizza
      (v), 102
Polenta Cakes, 29
Polenta Mountain, 132
Polenta Mountain Arrabbiata
    (v), 133
Potatoes
    Apples, Squash Soup, 44
    baking, 43
    Broccoli and Cheddar
      Soup, 51
    Carrot and Turnip Soup,
      50
    Corn Soup, 49
    Hearty Minestrone, 84
    Leek and Potato Soup, 43
    Lentil Soup, 48
    Patatas Bravas, 146
    Potatoes with Swiss Chard,
      149
    Russian Salad, 74
    Two-Color Potatoes, 153
    Veggie Burger, 129
    Warm Potato Salad, 75
Prunes
    Couscous with Prunes,
      120
    Granola Bars, 174
Puy lentils, 48. *See* Lentils

Q
Quesadillas, 19
Quiches
    Rice Quiche, 90
    Spinach Quiche, 92

R
Radicchio, 70
    Avocado Salad, 70
    Blue Cheese Salad, 81
Raisins
    Banana Muffins, 169
    Curry Couscous, 124
    Granola Bars, 174
    Oatmeal Cookies, 171
    Ricotta Coconut Cake,
      180

Raspberries
    Peach Melba Parfait (v),
      160
Ratatouille
    Lentil Ratatouille, 110
    Ratatouille with Bulgur
      (v), 121
Red Pasta, 116
Rhubarb, 165
    Strawberry Rhubarb
      Crumble, 165
Rice, 13
    Basmati Rice with Peas
      and Nuts, 154
    Rice Quiche, 90
    Rice Soup, 42
    Rice with Cranberries and
      Curry, 155
    Risotto with Sun-Dried
      Tomatoes, 85
    Vegetable Paella, 135
Ricotta cheese
    Ricotta Coconut Cake,
      180
    Spinach Quiche, 92
    Spinach Ricotta
      Cannelloni, 122
Rigatoni, Red Pasta, 116
Risotto with Sun-Dried
    Tomatoes, 85
Roasted Red Pepper Bread
    Salad (v), 77
Romano cheese
    Parmesan Baguette Bites
      (v), 25
Russian Salad, 74
Rutabaga
    Oven-Roasted Vegetables,
      152

S
Salads
    Asian Mandoline Salad (v),
      79
    Asian Salad, 62
    Avocado Salad, 70
    Blue Cheese Salad, 81
    Bread Salad, 77
    Chickpea Salad (v), 59
    Chicory Salad, 80
    Couscous Salad, 66
    Crispy Salad, 69
    Divine Salad, 68
    Greek Salad, 61
    Green Mango Salad (v), 76

Hearts of Palm Salad, 71
Hint of Orange Salad, 64
Legume Salad, 58
Lentil Salad, 59
Mandoline Salad, 79
Mango Salad, 76
Pasta and Brussels Sprouts
    Salad, 72
Pasta Salad with Basil
    Pesto, 73
Roasted Red Pepper
    Bread Salad (v), 77
Russian Salad, 74
Spaghetti Squash Salad, 78
Spanish Salad, 60
Tabbouleh, 67
Warm Potato Salad, 75
Wild Rice Salad, 65
Salsas
    Cilantro Salsa, 21
Sandwiches
    Club Sandwich, 97
    Grilled Vegetable
        Sandwiches, 88
    Sunny-Side Up Western
        Sandwiches, 89
    Tofu Pita Sandwiches, 93
Sauce
    Spaghetti Sauce, 112
Sesame seeds
    Asian Salad, 62
    Asparagus in Vinaigrette,
        140
    Banana Honey Fritters,
        158
    Bean Dip, 31
    Crispy Salad, 69
    Hint of Orange Salad, 64
    Lentil Pie, 86
    Mushroom Bites, 35
    toasting, 31
    Tofu Tacos, 113
Shallots, 98
    Cheese Fondue, 130
    Stuffed Tomato with Egg,
        98
    Stuffed Zucchini, 150
Shepherd's Pie
    Sweet Potato Shepherd's
        Pie, 131
Sides
    Asparagus in Vinaigrette,
        140
    Basmati Rice with Peas
        and Nuts, 154

Beans with Tomatoes, 142
Broccoli in Creamy Sauce,
    145
Cauliflower with Curry,
    144
Eggplant with Tomato, 151
Fragrant Carrots, 143
Lemony Artichokes, 141
Oven-Roasted Vegetables,
    152
Patatas Bravas, 146
Potatoes with Swiss Chard,
    149
Rice with Cranberries and
    Curry, 155
Stuffed Zucchini, 150
Sweet Potato Muffins, 147
Swiss Chard Gratin, 148
Two-Color Potatoes, 153
Snow peas
    Asian Salad, 62
Soups
    Broccoli and Cheddar
        Soup, 51
    Carrot and Turnip Soup,
        50
    Corn Soup, 49
    Gazpacho, 53
    Hearty Minestrone, 84
    Julienne Vegetable Soup,
        52
    Leek and Potato Soup, 43
    Lentil Soup, 48
    Mushroom Soup, 46
    Onion Soup, 45
    Pea Soup, 54
    Rice Soup, 42
    Squash Soup, 44
    Three-Bean Soup, 47
    Tofu Soup, 55
Sour cream
    Bean Dip, 31
    Curry Dip, 32
    Lentils with Cumin, 109
    Russian Salad, 74
    Stuffed Squash, 136
    Tofu Pita Sandwiches, 93
Soy milk
    Blueberry Muffins, 168
Spaghetti
    Frittata, 100
    Pecan Paradise Pasta, 119
Spaghetti Sauce, 112
Spaghetti Squash Salad, 78
Spanish Salad, 60

Spinach
    Asian Salad, 62
    Blue Cheese Salad, 81
    Blue Pasta, 115
    Chickpea Stew, 105
    Crispy Salad, 69
    Pasta Salad with Basil
        Pesto, 73
    Polenta Mountain, 132
    Roasted Pepper and Basil
        Cannelloni (v), 123
    Spinach Quiche, 92
    Spinach Ricotta
        Cannelloni, 122
    Vegetable Paella, 135
Sprouts, alfalfa
    Mandoline Salad, 79
Squash
    Couscous with Prunes,
        120
    Oven-Roasted Vegetables,
        152
    Spaghetti Squash Salad, 78
    Squash Soup, 44
    Stuffed Squash, 136
Strawberries
    Fruit Parfait, 160
    Fruit with Cream, 159
    Strawberry Mounds, 164
    Strawberry Rhubarb
        Crumble, 165
Stuffed Peppers, 137
Stuffed Squash, 136
Stuffed Tomato with Egg, 98
Stuffed Zucchini, 150
Sugar snap peas
    Asian Salad (v), 63
    Chicory Salad, 80
Sun-dried tomato pesto
    Double-Tomato Pesto
        Pizza (v), 103
    Sun-Dried Tomato Baked
        Camembert (v), 28
Sun-dried tomatoes
    Risotto with Sun-Dried
        Tomatoes, 85
Sunflower seeds
    Creamy Fruit Delight, 181
    Date Mini-Bites, 175
    Oatmeal Cookies, 171
    Rice with Cranberries and
        Curry, 155
    Veggie Burger, 129
Sunny-Side Up Western
    Sandwiches, 89

Sweet potatoes, 147
  Couscous with Prunes, 120
  Oven-Roasted Vegetables, 152
  Sweet Potato Muffins, 147
  Sweet Potato Shepherd's Pie, 131
  Two-Color Potatoes, 153
  Vegetable Curry, 128
Swiss chard
  Potatoes with Swiss Chard, 149
  Swiss Chard Gratin, 148
Swiss cheese
  Broccoli and Cheddar Soup (v), 51
  Cheese Fondue, 130
  Onion Pie, 87
  Sweet Potato Muffins, 147

T

Tabbouleh, 67
Tacos
  Tofu Tacos, 113
Tahini, 63
  Asian Salad, 62
  Hummus, 22
  Vegetable Stir-Fry, 127
  Veggie Burger, 129
Tamari, 13
  Asian Salad, 62
  Bagel Melt, 94
  Cauliflower Omelet, 95
  Club Sandwich, 97
  Curry Couscous, 124
  Green Pasta, 114
  Mushroom Bites, 35
  Sweet Potato Shepherd's Pie, 131
  Tofu Brochettes, 126
  Tofu Pita Sandwiches, 93
  Tofu Soup, 55
  Tofu Tacos, 113
  Tofu with Peanut Sauce, 125
  Vegetable Stir-Fry, 127
  Vegetarian Chop Suey, 134
Thai Red Curry Dip (v), 32
Three-Bean Omelet, 96
Three-Bean Soup, 47
Three-Fruit Salad, 161
Toasted Pita Chips, 23

Tofu, 14
  All-Dressed Pizza, 101
  Bagel Melt, 94
  Club Sandwich, 97
  Green Pasta, 114
  Mini Lasagnas, 106
  Mini Pitas with Eggs, 39
  Mushroom Bites, 35
  Spaghetti Sauce, 112
  Sweet Potato Shepherd's Pie, 131
  Tofu Brochettes, 126
  Tofu Cakes, 30
  Tofu Pita Sandwiches, 93
  Tofu Soup, 55
  Tofu Tacos, 113
  Tofu with Peanut Sauce, 125
  Vegetable Stir-Fry, 127
  Vegetarian Chop Suey, 134
  Veggie Burger, 129
Tomato juice
  Cilantro Salsa, 21
  Couscous Salad, 66
  Gazpacho, 53
Tomato sauce
  All-Dressed Pizza, 101
  Four-Cheese Pizza, 102
Tomatoes, 14
  Asian Salad, 62
  Bagel Melt, 94
  Beans with Tomatoes, 142
  Bread Salad, 77
  Bruschetta Baguette Bites, 26
  Burritos, 104
  Cherry Tomatoes with Cheese, 18
  Cherry Tomatoes with Zesty Cheese (v), 18
  Chickpea Stew, 105
  Chicory Salad, 80
  Chili sin Carne, 111
  Cilantro Salsa, 21
  Club Sandwich, 97
  Couscous with Prunes, 120
  Creamy Lentils, 108
  Cucumber, Gazpacho, 53
  Divine Salad, 68
  Eggplant with Tomato, 151
  Greek Salad, 61
  Grilled Vegetable Sandwiches, 88
  Guacamole, 20
  Hard-Boiled Eggs with

  Lentils, 99
  Hearts of Palm Salad, 71
  Hearty Minestrone, 84
  Legume Salad, 58
  Lentil Pie, 86
  Lentil Ratatouille, 110
  Lentil Salad, 59
  Lentil Soup, 48
  Lentils with Cumin, 109
  Macaroni with Tomato and Cheese, 118
  Mango Salad, 76
  Mini Lasagnas, 106
  Onion Pie, 87
  Pasta and Brussels Sprouts Salad, 72
  Pasta with Goat Cheese, 117
  Pesto Pizza, 103
  Polenta Cakes, 29
  Polenta Mountain, 132
  Quesadillas, 19
  Red Pasta, 116
  Rice Soup, 42
  Roasted Red Pepper Bread Salad (v), 77
  Spaghetti Sauce, 112
  Spaghetti Squash Salad, 78
  Spanish Salad, 60
  Stuffed Peppers, 137
  Stuffed Tomato with Egg, 98
  Stuffed Zucchini, 150
  Sunny-Side Up Western Sandwiches, 89
  Tabbouleh, 67
  Three-Bean Soup, 47
  Tofu Brochettes, 126
  Tofu Cakes, 30
  Tofu Tacos, 113
  Vegetable Paella, 135
  Wild Rice Salad, 65
Tortillas
  Burritos, 104
  Pesto Pizza, 103
  Quesadillas, 19
  Vegetable Roll-Ups, 38
Turnips
  Broccoli and Cheddar Soup, 51
  Carrot and Turnip Soup, 50
  Chickpea Stew, 105
  Couscous with Prunes, 120
  Two-Color Potatoes, 153

V

Vacherin des Bois Francs
    cheese, 94
Vegetable broth, 14, 50
    Broccoli and Cheddar
        Soup, 51
    Carrot and Turnip Soup,
        50
    Corn Soup, 49
    Hearty Minestrone, 84
    Julienne Vegetable Soup, 52
    Leek and Potato Soup, 43
    Mushroom Soup, 46
    Onion Soup, 45
    Pea Soup, 54
    Rice Soup, 42
    Risotto with Sun-Dried
        Tomatoes, 85
    Squash Soup, 44
    Three-Bean Soup, 47
    Tofu Soup, 55
    Vegetable Curry, 128
    Vegetable Paella, 135
Vegetable Curry, 128
Vegetable Paella, 135
Vegetable Roll-Ups, 38
Vegetable Stir-Fry, 127
Vegetarian Chop Suey, 134
Veggie Burger, 129
Vermicelli. *See also* Pasta
    Julienne Vegetable Soup, 52
    Tofu Soup, 55
Vinegars, 14

W

Walnuts
    Chocolate Chip Cookies,
        172

Grandmother's Sugar Pie,
    177
Oatmeal Cookies, 171
Warm Potato Salad, 75
Watermelon
    Three-Fruit Salad, 161
Whole grains, 14
Wild Rice Salad, 65
Wild rice, 15
    Wild Rice Salad, 65

Y

Yogurt
    Blueberry Muffins, 168
    Chickpea Stew, 105
    Creamy Fruit Delight,
        181
    Date Mini-Bites, 175
    Fruit Parfait, 160
    Mini Pitas with Eggs, 39
    Pineapple Muffins, 166
    Thai Red Curry Dip (v),
        32
    Warm Potato Salad (v),
        75

Z

Zesty Four-Cheese Pizza (v),
    102
Zucchini
    All-Dressed Pizza, 101
    Asian Salad, 62
    Chili sin Carne, 111
    Corn Soup, 49
    Couscous Salad (v), 66
    Couscous with Prunes,
        120
    Creamy Lentils, 108
    Feta Cheese Bites, 37

Green Pasta, 114
Grilled Vegetable
    Sandwiches, 88
Hearty Minestrone, 84
Julienne Vegetable Soup,
    52
Legume Salad, 58
Lentil Ratatouille, 110
Lentils with Cumin, 109
Pasta and Brussels Sprouts
    Salad, 72
Pasta with Goat Cheese,
    117
Polenta Mountain, 132
Quesadillas, 19
Rice Quiche, 90
Rice Soup, 42
Roasted Red Pepper Mini
    Lasagnas (v), 107
Spaghetti Sauce, 112
Spaghetti Squash Salad,
    78
Stuffed Squash, 136
Stuffed Zucchini, 150
Sweet Potato Muffins,
    147
Sweet Potato Shepherd's
    Pie, 131
Tofu Brochettes, 126
Tofu Pita Sandwiches, 93
Tofu Tacos, 113
Vegetable Curry, 128
Vegetable Roll-Ups, 38
Vegetarian Chop Suey,
    134
Warm Potato Salad, 75
Zucchini Roasted Red
    Pepper Mini Lasagnas
    (v), 107

Also Available
from Robert Rose

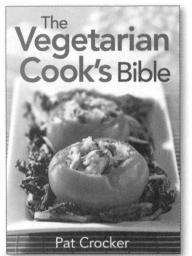
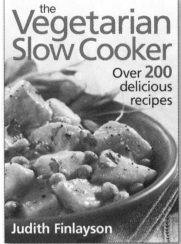
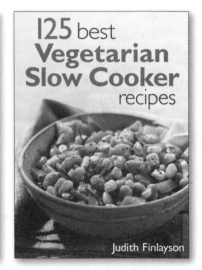

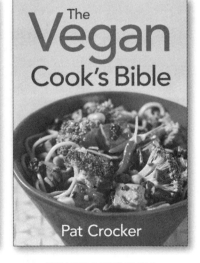